The
Pinkprint

Also from EATMS Productions

Books on power, survival, women's autonomy, and the systems shaping modern America.

Modern Rewrites for Women

Stoic Principles Reimagined
Siddhartha Reimagined
The Prince Reimagined for Women
The Art of War Reimagined for Women
The Jungle Reimagined
The Constitution Reimagined for Women

Machine Learning Series

AI, Bitcoin, Nostr for Women
AI, Safety, & Security for Women
AI, Anxiety, & Health for Women
AI, Kids, & Family Safety for Women
AI, Creativity, & Personal Expression for Women
AI, Independent Work, & Parallel Power for Women

Social Systems Series

Emotional Labor for Women
Household Power for Women
Workplace Power for Women
Medical Bias for Women
Aging Systems for Women
Recovery Systems for Women

Fiction
Dystopian Stories of Resistance and Collapse

Propaganda Paige & the Missing Prosperity
Propaganda Paige & the TIDE Manifesto
Propaganda Paige & the Shadow Cartographers
Propaganda Paige & the Prosperity Alliance
Propaganda Paige & the Shattered Truth
Propaganda Paige & the Rising TIDE
Propaganda Paige & the Last Bastion
Propaganda Paige & the Dawn of Prosperity
Project 2025: Dorian — The Last Men
Project 2025: Boy — A Last Men Novel

Fascism, Project 2025, & The Pinkprint

A Progressive Vision Not The Regressive One

(introducing TIDE)

Our Future 1

by
Esme Mees
& Luna Max

EATMS
PRODUCTIONS

ISBN: 979-8-9909279-2-6

Cover, interior design, interior prints by: Esme Mees

www.eatms.me
eatms@pm.me

Printed in the United States of America.

You may not be able to alter reality, but you can alter your attitude towards it, and this, paradoxically, alters reality. Try it and see.

— Margaret Atwood

Fascism is a far-right, authoritarian political ideology characterized by dictatorial power, suppression of dissent, and strong regimentation of society and the economy, often combined with an emphasis on nationalism, militarism, and the glorification of a single leader or party.

Key features include:

Authoritarianism: Centralized control with limited personal freedoms.

Nationalism: Intense pride in and promotion of a homogeneous national identity, often at the expense of marginalized groups.

Suppression of Opposition: Censorship, propaganda, and violence are used to silence critics.

Economic Control: Collaboration between the state and private enterprise, with policies favoring corporate and elite interests over the public.

Cult of Personality: Devotion to a leader who is portrayed as infallible and the savior of the nation.

Use of Violence: State-sanctioned or tacitly approved violence is often employed to intimidate, oppress, and eliminate opposition, creating a climate of fear that reinforces authoritarian control.

As exemplified in the policies of *Project 2025* and the broader Republican agenda, fascist tendencies can be identified in efforts to curtail civil liberties, impose regressive social policies, and consolidate power through fear-mongering and scapegoating. These agendas often exploit societal divisions and prioritize the interests of the elite, while masking authoritarian control as the preservation of "freedom" and "traditional values."

Table of Contents

The Blueprint

Project 2025 is a collection of fascist far right "Christian" nationalist policy proposals designed to overhaul the U.S. government. Created by the Heritage Foundation, implemented as a theocratic extreme Republican agenda, this monstrous plan, 920 pages, aims to push a radical "Christian" nationalist agenda, stripping rights and protections. It is a nightmare scenario for democracy, civil liberties, international relations, and the environment.

Here is their plan-

Mandate for Leadership
The Conservative Promise
Project 2025: Presidential Transition Project

10

The Pinkprint

The Pinkprint is a progressive vision to counteract the authoritarian fantasies of far-right "Christian" nationalism. While the Heritage Foundation's regressive blueprint dreams of a nation shackled by radicalism, the Pinkprint charts a path to justice, equity, and true democracy. This plan reclaims the values of compassion, community, and environmental stewardship, challenging every dystopian policy with solutions rooted in liberation and progress. It is a roadmap to safeguard civil liberties, protect our planet, and honor the dignity of all people, not just the powerful few.

Here is our plan-

Pinkprint for Progress
The Progressive Commitment
Project 2025: Vision for a Just Transition

The TIDE is a Turning!

Foreword: TIDE
A Vision for America

- A Modern Tale, Finally

Gather round, everyone, for the story you are about to hear is more hopeful than what has ever come before. "Forward: TIDE- A Vision for America" is not just a title; it is how we reclaim end fascism, democracy, and building a society rooted in justice, equity, and freedom. Rather than a political shift that deepens divisions or consolidates oppressive power, this vision represents a bold transformation toward a nation that champions liberation over domination. It offers a framework for dismantling systems of greed and authoritarianism, replacing them with structures that empower communities, protect civil liberties, and foster global cooperation. This is not a terrifying prospect but an inspiring call to action, a promise to build a future where democracy thrives, human rights are sacrosanct, and progress uplifts everyone, not just the privileged fascist few.

The Secular Revival

Let's start with one of the most essential pillars of a just society: the preservation of secular governance. *The Pinkprint* envisions a government that honors true religious freedom, freedom for all . beliefs and for those who choose none, not a fascist regime where one narrow interpretation of faith dominates public life. This is about restoring the separation of church and state, ensuring that no dogma can override individual rights or the democratic principles enshrined in the Constitution. Imagine a nation where policies are crafted to serve the common good, guided by reason, equity, and justice, not the rigid dictates of exclusionary morality. In this vision, diversity of thought and belief is celebrated, and every citizen is empowered to live without fear of marginalization or oppression simply for being who they are. It's not just about safeguarding rights, it's about building a society where those rights flourish.

Democratic Empowerment

The Pinkprint champions a vision where power is decentralized, shared, and held accountable, a sharp departure from any model that seeks to consolidate authority in the hands of a few. Democracy thrives when checks and balances are preserved, when no single branch or leader can act unilaterally, and when every voice is heard, not silenced. This vision ensures that appointments to public office reflect the diversity and needs of the nation, not the loyalty to an agenda. Imagine a government where transparency and oversight are standard practices, where decisions affecting millions are made through open debate and collective wisdom. In this future, dissent is not a threat but a vital part of the democratic process, ensuring that power remains accountable to the people it serves. This is a nation built on collaboration, dialogue, and the understanding that true strength lies in shared governance, not authoritarian control.

Economic and Social Renewal

The Pinkprint envisions an economy that works for everyone, not just the wealthy few. Instead of policies that widen inequality, we advocate for a system where prosperity is shared and dignity is a universal right. This means robust regulations that protect workers, consumers, and the environment from exploitation. Public services like healthcare and education remain public, accessible to all as foundational rights rather than commodities reserved for those who can afford them. Living wages, fair labor practices, and expanded worker protections ensure that no one is left behind in the pursuit of progress. Imagine an economy where communities thrive, not just corporations; where taxes on the wealthiest fund vital infrastructure and social programs, lifting millions out of poverty. In this vision, economic growth is not measured by profits alone but by the well-being of the people who drive it. It's a future where fairness and opportunity replace greed and exclusion, a true renewal of America's promise.

Social Progress and Inclusion

The Pinkprint champions a society where everyone's rights are not only protected but celebrated as essential to the fabric of democracy. Women's autonomy over their bodies and reproductive health is non-negotiable, with access to abortion and contraception safeguarded as fundamental healthcare rights. LGBTQ+ individuals are embraced with policies that ensure full protections, eradicating discrimination in all its forms. True religious freedom means no one's beliefs are used as a weapon to deny others dignity, access, or opportunity. Businesses and service providers will serve all people equally, fostering inclusion over exclusion. Imagine living in a society where rights and liberties are expansive, not conditional, where your freedom is not limited by someone else's beliefs, but instead upheld by shared respect for diversity. This is a vision of progress, compassion, and the unwavering belief that equality strengthens us all.

Environmental Stewardship and Renewal

The Pinkprint envisions a future where environmental policies prioritize the health of the planet and the well-being of all who inhabit it. Instead of deregulation and exploitation, this vision calls for bold climate action that invests in renewable energy, protects public lands, and promotes sustainable practices. Fossil fuels give way to clean energy innovations that not only combat climate change but create jobs and strengthen local economies. Public lands are preserved as national treasures, ensuring that they remain untouched by private interests and accessible to all. Internationally, the U.S. leads in climate cooperation, recommitting to agreements that address global challenges and foster solutions. Imagine a world where forests thrive, oceans are clean, and the air we breathe is safe for generations to come. This is not just environmental protection; it is a renewal of our collective responsibility to live in harmony with the earth and one another.

Global Leadership Through Cooperation

The Pinkprint envisions a United States that leads not with aggression but with diplomacy, collaboration, and a commitment to global justice. Instead of escalating conflicts or funneling resources into unchecked militarization, this vision prioritizes investment in social programs, humanitarian aid, and sustainable development at home and abroad. Foreign policy becomes a tool for building bridges, not walls, fostering international partnerships to address shared challenges like climate change, poverty, and human rights. The U.S. reclaims its role as a champion of peace and democracy, promoting dialogue and understanding over domination. Imagine a world where America's influence uplifts rather than oppresses, where cooperation replaces coercion, and where strength is measured by the alliances we build, not the conflicts we provoke. This is the path toward a stable and just global community, grounded in mutual respect and shared progress.

Protecting the Freedom to Dissent
The Pinkprint champions the fundamental right to dissent as a cornerstone of democracy. Rather than suppressing opposing voices, this vision ensures that every individual has the freedom to speak, assemble, and protest without fear of retaliation. Independent media thrives, free from corporate or political interference, creating a platform for diverse perspectives and robust public debate. Social media becomes a tool for connection and accountability, fostering transparency and amplifying marginalized voices. Laws and policies protect, rather than punish, those who speak out against injustice, ensuring that public assembly and peaceful protest remain sacrosanct. Imagine a society where dissent is not silenced but celebrated as an act of civic engagement, where activism is met with dialogue, not suppression, and where the government serves its people by listening to their voices, not stifling them. This is a vision of democracy that empowers, not intimidates.

Conclusion
The Pinkprint: TIDE – A Vision for America offers a powerful alternative to the oppressive ambitions outlined in regressive blueprints. Instead of dismantling democracy, it fortifies it. Rather than centralizing power, it redistributes it to the people. This vision rejects rigid hierarchies in favor of equity and inclusion, ensuring that all voices contribute to the social order. Domestically, it protects the environment, advances social justice, and invests in the well-being of communities. Globally, it fosters cooperation and peace, promoting stability and shared progress. *The Pinkprint* isn't just a plan, it's a commitment to a future where democracy thrives, humanity flourishes, and the promise of justice becomes a reality for all.

TIDE: Target, Inspire, Disrupt, Empower

Each pillar, Target, Inspire, Disrupt, Empower, represents a step in building a future rooted in equity, justice, and sustainability. Together, these principles form the foundation for a movement that opposes fascism, oppression, and creates lasting change.

Target identifies the core systems, institutions, and individuals responsible for perpetuating inequality and harm. Whether it's corporations funding destructive policies, lawmakers blocking progress, or systems exploiting marginalized communities, targeting shines a spotlight on these forces, holding them accountable. It ensures that the fight for justice is focused, strategic, and unrelenting.

Inspire reminds us that no movement can thrive without hope and connection. Storytelling, art, and collective action ignite passion and solidarity, transforming despair into determination. Inspiration is the fuel for progress, reminding us why we fight and what we can achieve together.

Disrupt recognizes that oppressive systems rely on compliance. By disrupting their rhythms, through boycotts, strikes, protests, and civil disobedience, we expose their fragility. Disruption is not chaos; it is a calculated refusal to accept the status quo, a strategic challenge to entrenched power.

Empower is the culmination of TIDE, focusing on creating systems that uplift and sustain communities. Empowerment ensures that as we dismantle unjust structures, we build resilient alternatives: participatory democracy, mutual aid networks, and inclusive governance. It is the process of returning power to the people, ensuring that progress is not temporary but permanent.

TIDE is a clear and aggressive plan to tear down systems built on greed and oppression. Politicians have proven, time after time, that they cannot be trusted. They choose greed and self-interest over the people they are supposed to represent. TIDE demands we target the roots of injustice, inspire people to act together, disrupt the power structures that keep us oppressed, and empower communities to take control of their own futures. The ultimate goal is to eliminate the need for politicians altogether, replacing them with technology that allows us to govern ourselves, fairly, transparently, and directly. Liberation is not a dream; it is the path we are building.

Reclaim Direct Democracy: Defund Congress

The Pinkprint envisions a future where governance belongs to the people, free from the inefficiencies and corruptions of the current congressional system. Congress, as it operates today, often stands as a barrier to progress, a structure entrenched in outdated norms and dominated by corporate lobbying and partisan power plays. Rather than serving as a tool for democracy, it has become a bottleneck, where the interests of the few override the needs of the many. In this vision, we oppose this stagnation by redefining governance itself, using technology to create a decentralized, transparent, and participatory democracy that bypasses traditional gatekeepers.

The foundation of this transformation lies in dismantling the financial and institutional grip that allows Congress to operate as a machine for special interests rather than public good. By defunding the excessive mechanisms that perpetuate congressional power, such as exorbitant campaign financing, lobbyist influence, and outsized administrative costs, we shift resources back to the people. This doesn't mean dismantling governance altogether; it means reallocating its purpose. Funds previously tied to maintaining the status quo can be redirected toward technological infrastructure that enables direct citizen engagement in decision-making. Imagine a system where policy is not dictated by a handful of lawmakers but actively shaped by millions of voices in real time.

This evolution hinges on technology. Secure platforms, built on blockchain and other decentralized systems, can facilitate direct voting, policy proposals, and public discourse, ensuring that every citizen has a tangible role in governance. These platforms would eliminate concerns of fraud or manipulation, using encrypted verification systems to authenticate identities while protecting privacy. Every citizen, regardless of socioeconomic status, would have equal access to shaping the laws that govern their lives. In this model, Congress no longer serves as the sole legislative body; it becomes obsolete, replaced by a participatory democracy that is as dynamic and adaptable as the people it serves.

Critics may argue that direct democracy at this scale is impractical, citing concerns over misinformation, low engagement, or logistical challenges. *The Pinkprint* acknowledges these obstacles but frames them as opportunities for innovation, not excuses for inaction. A robust framework for civic education will accompany this technological shift, ensuring that citizens are equipped with the knowledge to engage meaningfully. Transparent algorithms and independent oversight can guard against misinformation campaigns, while gamification and incentives encourage participation. The goal is not just a functional system but an engaged citizenry empowered to shape its collective destiny.

This vision is not a call for chaos but a demand for accountability. Traditional representative systems often centralize power in ways that make it difficult for citizens to hold leaders accountable. Direct democracy disperses power, returning it to the hands of the people. With no intermediaries, there is no room for the influence of corporate lobbyists or backroom deals. Policies are debated openly, decisions are made collectively, and power flows from the ground up. The act of opposing corruption becomes built into the system itself.

At its heart, this shift represents more than a technical upgrade to governance, it is a philosophical revolution. It challenges the assumption that a small group of elected officials can adequately represent the will of an entire population. Instead, it affirms that the collective wisdom of engaged citizens, equipped with the right tools and education, can govern more effectively and equitably. This is not a rejection of democracy but its evolution, where representation is replaced with participation, and leadership becomes about facilitation rather than control.

The Pinkprint's vision of direct democracy is not only achievable but necessary in the face of entrenched inequality and systemic failures. By opposing the inefficiencies and inequities of the current system, we open the door to a government that reflects the true will of the people. Defunding Congress as it stands today is not about dismantling democracy, it is about liberating it, transforming governance from a distant institution into a living, participatory process. Together, through innovation and collective action, we will build a system where power is not hoarded but shared, where decisions are not dictated but debated, and where democracy is not a privilege but a right. Ending fascism starts with ending greed.

Section 1:
Taking the Reins of Government
1 White House Office
Compassion over Greed

- A Once Upon a Soon Time Tale

Attention please! What is about to be revealed will leave you speechless and utterly delighted. "Taking the Reins of Government: White House Office," in *The Pinkprint* is a vision for using the highest office in the land as a force for equity, justice, and transformation. Rather than a guide to consolidating power for authoritarian ends, this section reimagines the presidency as a platform for servant leadership, a model of governance that prioritizes compassion, collaboration, and transparency. The White House is no longer a symbol of dominance but a cornerstone for building a government of, by, and for the people, fully committed to uplifting the most marginalized voices and addressing systemic inequities.

The White House is more than an office; it is the symbol of a nation's identity, its promise, and its values. Under *The Pinkprint*, it transforms into the beating heart of a progressive future, one rooted in compassion and collective responsibility. Leadership by compassion is not about weakness or pandering to sentimentality; it is about seeing governance as a moral obligation to serve the people, to uplift the vulnerable, and to forge a society where no one is left behind. This is not leadership for its own sake or the consolidation of power for those who already have too much. It is leadership as service, fierce, clear-eyed, and resolute in its commitment to justice.

At its core, the White House becomes a place of radical transparency and human connection. Imagine a presidency where the voices of everyday citizens, not lobbyists or corporations, dictate the course of the nation. Town halls replace closed-door meetings; public accountability becomes the foundation, not an afterthought. Policies are crafted with empathy, informed by lived experience, and rooted in the realities of those too often ignored. Decisions are no longer filtered through layers of bureaucracy designed to obscure and delay but are made swiftly, boldly, and in direct response to the needs of the people.

Compassionate leadership does not shy away from hard truths; it confronts them. The White House of *The Pinkprint* tackles systemic inequality head-on, recognizing that the presidency is not a pedestal but a platform. It is the nexus where the struggles of workers, mothers, students, and communities converge and where real, actionable solutions are forged. This administration would prioritize dismantling systemic racism, addressing gender inequality, and protecting the rights of all citizens, especially those historically oppressed. This means more than symbolic gestures; it means real investment in education, housing, healthcare, and climate justice.

Gone are the days when the White House is a fortress of elitism and secrecy. Under *The Pinkprint*, its walls become porous, metaphorically speaking, inviting in the voices of those who were once shut out. Leaders listen not just to the powerful but to the teachers, farmers, nurses, and organizers who truly drive the nation forward. There are no empty promises of bipartisanship when one side is fighting for survival and the other for profit. Instead, this presidency demands bold action that puts people first, above profit margins, above political maneuvering, and above personal gain.

Leadership by compassion requires reimagining the role of power itself. The president is not a ruler but a steward, one who understands that authority is not a privilege but a responsibility. This vision does not entertain platitudes of neutrality or the false comfort of incremental change. It acts decisively, knowing that every delay in addressing poverty, healthcare access, or climate catastrophe costs lives. Compassion is not passive; it is active, relentless, and unyielding. It insists on a government that values people over corporations, sustainability over short-term profits, and community over individualism.

The White House of *The Pinkprint* is also a hub for innovation, not in the sterile, profit-driven sense but as a crucible for creative solutions to society's most pressing problems. It welcomes thinkers, activists, and visionaries from across the nation and the globe, harnessing collective wisdom to tackle the challenges that no single person or party can solve alone. This is where the brightest ideas converge, not to serve the interests of a select few but to uplift everyone. From climate scientists to community organizers, the administration seeks voices that challenge, question, and inspire.

Critically, the presidency under *The Pinkprint* restores dignity to public service. The people staffing the White House are not career politicians climbing a ladder or corporate players seeking influence; they are individuals deeply committed to public good. Salaries are capped, conflicts of interest are eradicated, and the revolving door between government and industry is slammed shut. This administration is staffed by nurses, teachers, and environmentalists, people who know the value of hard work and the stakes of failure.

Finally, the White House sets the tone for a global shift toward justice. Compassionate leadership recognizes that America does not exist in a vacuum. The decisions made in Washington ripple across the globe, affecting ecosystems, economies, and communities far beyond its borders. The *Pinkprint* presidency commits to international cooperation, prioritizing diplomacy over dominance and sustainability over exploitation. It leads by example, showing that a government rooted in empathy and equity is not only possible but necessary.

This is not the White House as we know it. This is the White House as it should be: a place where power is wielded not for the benefit of a few but for the liberation of all. It is a symbol of a nation unafraid to embrace compassion as strength, to see governance as a collective endeavor, and to lead with purpose, clarity, and heart. This is leadership by compassion, and this is the America we are building.

Section 1:
Taking the Reins of Government
2 Executive Office of the President of the United States
Governance for the People

- A Once Upon a Soon Time Tale

The good dream continues and is very real. "Taking the Reins of
Leadership: Executive Office of the President," under *The Pinkprint*
envisions a progressive transformation of governance, where the
executive branch becomes a model of transparency, collaboration,
and service to the people. Rather than consolidating power for
ideological control, this approach decentralizes authority,
strengthens federal agencies, and ensures that governance reflects
the diverse needs of the nation. It prioritizes democratic principles,
fostering a system where checks and balances are not just preserved
but enhanced to hold leadership accountable and protect the rights
of all citizens.

This vision centers on a radical reimagining of the Executive Office
of the President, where power is not hoarded but shared, and
governance is a collective act of service to the people. Under *The
Pinkprint,* the Executive Office becomes a beacon of empowerment,
collaboration, and accountability. It is no longer a top-down
authority issuing directives in isolation but a dynamic network
where the expertise of communities and professionals within federal
agencies shapes every decision. Policy is no longer the domain of a
select few disconnected from the realities of the people they serve.
Instead, it becomes a living, evolving process informed by the
experiences, insights, and struggles of the many.

Efficiency is not achieved by dismantling oversight or silencing
dissent. These are the tools of authoritarianism, designed to create
the illusion of progress while stripping away the core of democracy.
The Pinkprint rejects these shortcuts. Instead, efficiency is redefined as
responsiveness, streamlining processes not to bypass checks and
balances but to ensure that government actions are swift, equitable,
and effective. It is about cutting red tape without cutting corners,
reducing bureaucracy without reducing accountability. Every
process is measured against a single standard: does this serve the

people, or does it serve the system? If the answer is the latter, it is reworked or removed.

At the heart of this reimagined Executive Office is the principle of loyalty, not loyalty to a rigid ideology or to the preservation of power, but loyalty to justice, equity, and inclusivity. These principles guide every decision, from how policies are crafted to how resources are allocated. Under *The Pinkprint*, loyalty to the public good replaces the backroom deals and partisan loyalty tests that have plagued governance for decades. There is no room for self-interest or the interests of a privileged few. The only agenda is the collective welfare of the nation.

The Executive Office becomes a hub of collaboration, where diverse voices come together to craft policies that serve everyone. Experts are no longer sidelined by political appointees with agendas; instead, their knowledge and experience are the foundation of every decision. Scientists guide environmental policies, educators shape education reform, and healthcare professionals lead public health initiatives. Advocacy groups, community leaders, and citizens are invited into the process, ensuring that the policies reflect the needs and aspirations of those they impact the most.

Collaboration does not mean chaos. It means creating systems where every voice can be heard without being drowned out. Technology plays a key role, enabling real-time feedback, secure public engagement, and transparent decision-making. Citizens can see how their input is used, building trust and fostering a sense of ownership over the policies that govern their lives. This is governance that listens, not just during election years but every day, in every action it takes. It is a government that adapts to the evolving needs of its people, unafraid to admit when it has fallen short and committed to doing better.

This vision transforms the Executive Office into a force for good that bridges the divide between government and the people. Trust, long eroded by corruption, greed, and inefficiency, is rebuilt through transparency and action. The public sees not just words but results: clean water, safe neighborhoods, thriving schools, and opportunities that are no longer reserved for the privileged. The office becomes a place of hope, where the promise of democracy is fulfilled not through empty rhetoric but through tangible change.

Under *The Pinkprint*, the Executive Office is also a space for innovation. It recognizes that the challenges of the 21st century demand new solutions, not recycled ideas from the past. Climate change, economic inequality, systemic racism, these are not problems that can be solved by outdated methods. The office embraces forward-thinking approaches, drawing on the best ideas from around the world and adapting them to the unique needs of the nation. It invests in renewable energy, universal broadband, and public transportation that connects communities rather than dividing them. It fosters a culture of creativity, where failure is seen not as a setback but as a step toward progress.

But perhaps most importantly, this vision lays the foundation for a government that is truly of, by, and for the people. It recognizes that power does not belong in the hands of a few but must be distributed widely and equitably. The Executive Office under *The Pinkprint* is not an ivory tower but a bridge, connecting federal agencies, local governments, and the communities they serve. It decentralizes decision-making, empowering states, cities, and towns to tailor solutions to their unique challenges while providing the resources and support they need to succeed.

Leadership in this model is not about domination; it is about facilitation. The Executive Office does not dictate; it listens, guides, and collaborates. It sees its role not as the final arbiter of power but as a steward of democracy, ensuring that every voice is heard and every need is met. This is a government that evolves with its people, one that understands that progress is not a destination but a continuous journey.

The White House, under this vision, becomes a symbol of what is possible when power is used not to control but to liberate. It is a place where the ideals of equity, inclusivity, and justice are not just aspirations but lived realities. It embodies a government that works for everyone, not just the few. This is the America we are building, a nation where leadership is not a privilege but a responsibility, where governance is not about power but about people, and where democracy is not just preserved but reimagined for a better future.

Section 1:
Taking the Reins of Government
3 Central Personnel Agencies: Managing the Bureaucracy Empowering the Workforce

- A Once Upon a Soon Time Tale

Everyone, hold on, because this is going to be deeply hopeful. "Taking the Reins of Leadership: Central Personnel Agencies," under *The Pinkprint* is a bold blueprint for transforming the federal workforce into a model of equity, efficiency, and service. Rather than overhauling the administrative state to consolidate power, this vision prioritizes empowering public servants to create a government that works for everyone. It focuses on fostering a culture of collaboration, innovation, and accountability within federal agencies, ensuring they are equipped to meet the needs of the nation with fairness and transparency. This is not about dismantling bureaucracy for ideological control; it is about reimagining it as a system that reflects the best of what public service can be.

The heart of any government is its people, those who work behind the scenes, day after day, ensuring the machinery of the state runs smoothly. Under *The Pinkprint,* the federal workforce becomes more than a tool of governance; it becomes a driving force for equity, justice, and progress. "Taking the Reins of Leadership: Central Personnel Agencies" reimagines the role of public servants, not as faceless bureaucrats serving an outdated system, but as empowered agents of change shaping a government that works for everyone. This is a vision where central personnel agencies are no longer instruments of control or efficiency at any cost but hubs of collaboration, innovation, and transparency.

At the core of this transformation is a fundamental shift in how federal employees are treated and valued. Bureaucracy, as it currently exists, is often seen as a tangled web of inefficiency and frustration. But *The Pinkprint* recognizes the untapped potential within these systems. Public servants are not obstacles to progress; they are its architects. For decades, the workforce has been undermined, resources slashed, morale drained, and expertise ignored in favor of political appointments and corporate contracts.

This vision seeks to undo that damage, rebuilding a workforce that is motivated, skilled, and respected.

Empowering the federal workforce begins with treating its members with the dignity they deserve. This means fair pay, comprehensive benefits, and workplace protections that rival any in the private sector. Too often, public servants are asked to do more with less, shouldering the weight of a nation's needs while enduring stagnant wages and diminished job security. *The Pinkprint* envisions a future where federal employment is not just a calling but a career of choice, one that attracts the brightest minds and the most passionate hearts. These individuals are not cogs in a machine; they are innovators, problem-solvers, and advocates for the public good.

This transformation also involves redefining how agencies operate and interact with one another. Silos and red tape have long plagued the administrative state, creating inefficiencies that frustrate both employees and the public they serve. *The Pinkprint* calls for streamlined processes that prioritize collaboration and flexibility. Imagine a federal workforce where agencies share resources, expertise, and data seamlessly, working together to address complex challenges. This is not about stripping agencies of their autonomy but fostering a culture of cooperation that amplifies their collective impact.

Central personnel agencies play a pivotal role in ensuring this vision becomes reality. These agencies become the architects of a fair and inclusive hiring process, one that prioritizes diversity and equity at every level. Under this model, recruitment focuses not on connections or credentials alone but on skills, lived experiences, and the ability to contribute meaningfully to public service. This means removing barriers that have historically excluded marginalized communities, ensuring that the federal workforce reflects the diversity of the nation it serves. Representation is not a buzzword; it is a necessity.

Training and development also take center stage in this reimagined workforce. *The Pinkprint* invests in ongoing education and professional growth, recognizing that the challenges of governance are ever-evolving. Employees are equipped with the tools they need to succeed, from cutting-edge technology to leadership development programs. But this isn't about creating a workforce of technocrats; it's about nurturing a culture of learning and adaptability, where every employee feels empowered to innovate and take initiative. Mistakes are not punished but treated as opportunities for growth, fostering an environment where creativity thrives.

Transparency and accountability are the cornerstones of this vision. The federal workforce operates in service to the public, and every action it takes must reflect that commitment. Under *The Pinkprint*, central personnel agencies establish clear standards of accountability, ensuring that public servants act with integrity and that misconduct is addressed swiftly and fairly. But accountability is a two-way street. Just as employees are held to high standards, they are also protected from undue political influence and retaliation. Whistleblower protections are strengthened, creating a system where individuals can speak out against corruption and injustice without fear of reprisal.

Perhaps most importantly, this vision redefines the relationship between the federal workforce and the people it serves. The public often views bureaucracy as a monolith, an impenetrable fortress of inefficiency. *The Pinkprint* seeks to break down those walls, creating a government that is accessible, responsive, and transparent. Central personnel agencies lead the charge, establishing mechanisms for direct communication between public servants and citizens. Whether it's through digital platforms, community forums, or public reporting systems, these agencies ensure that the voices of the people are not just heard but acted upon.

This is not governance as usual; it is governance reimagined. It recognizes that a government is only as strong as the people who run it and that the people who run it are only as strong as the systems that support them. Central personnel agencies under *The Pinkprint* are no longer tools of enforcement or oversight alone, they are engines of empowerment, driving a government that works not just for the people but with them.

The federal workforce is not the problem; it is the solution. And under *The Pinkprint*, it will finally be given the resources, respect, and responsibility it needs to lead the way into a brighter, fairer future.

Section 2:
The Common Defense Fund
4 Department of Defense
Global Peace and Resilience Fund

- A Once Upon a Soon Time Tale

Citizens of the world, brace yourselves, because what you are about to hear will send tingles up your spine. "The Common Defense Fund: Department of Defense," under *The Pinkprint* envisions a transformative approach to reimagining America's military and its role in fostering global peace and stability. Rather than narrowly defining national security through aggressive strategies and budgetary excesses, this vision prioritizes diplomacy, sustainability, and collaboration as the cornerstones of defense. Under *The Pinkprint,* the Department of Defense becomes a force not for domination but for protection, advancing global cooperation and long-term stability.

The *Pinkprint's* vision for the Department of Defense begins with a fundamental shift in how we define national security. For too long, security has been treated as synonymous with military dominance, an endless arms race that prioritizes firepower over foresight. This approach, while profitable for defense contractors and their lobbyists, has done little to create lasting peace or stability. Instead, it has drained resources, fueled conflict, and perpetuated cycles of fear and violence. Under *The Pinkprint,* national security is no longer a reactionary endeavor focused solely on immediate threats. It becomes a proactive commitment to addressing the deeper causes of insecurity, poverty, inequality, environmental degradation, and fostering a world where true safety is possible.

At the heart of this transformation is the recognition that bloated defense budgets serve interests other than those of the people. Trillions of dollars have been funneled into projects that enrich private companies while neglecting the real needs of communities. Schools crumble, healthcare remains inaccessible, and infrastructure fails, all while billions are spent on weapons systems designed for wars that may never come. *The Pinkprint* reimagines this system entirely, slashing unnecessary expenditures and redirecting funds to initiatives that strengthen the foundations of security: education, housing, renewable energy, and global partnerships that prioritize human well-being over military might.

This reallocation of resources is not a retreat, it is a redefinition of strength. A nation is not strong because of the number of missiles it stockpiles or the size of its defense contracts. Strength is found in the resilience of its people, the health of its environment, and the stability of its alliances. *The Pinkprint* rejects the false dichotomy that pits domestic well-being against international security. Instead, it acknowledges that these priorities are interconnected. A community with access to education, clean water, and economic opportunities is far less likely to face conflict, both internally and externally. By investing in these areas, we create a ripple effect that enhances security far beyond our borders.

Central to this vision is the shift from aggression to diplomacy. The Department of Defense, under *The Pinkprint,* becomes not just a military institution but a leader in fostering global cooperation. Diplomacy is not an afterthought; it is the first and most important tool of national security. This means expanding the role of diplomats, negotiators, and peacebuilders within the defense ecosystem. Instead of sending soldiers to every corner of the globe, we send aid workers, educators, and environmental experts who can address the root causes of instability. The focus shifts from preparing for war to preventing it, from posturing to problem-solving.

This approach also requires rethinking how the military engages with the global community. Partnerships with other nations are no longer based on power imbalances or coercive tactics but on mutual respect and shared goals. Alliances are built not to dominate but to collaborate, addressing global challenges like climate change, refugee crises, and pandemics. By working alongside international organizations and non-governmental groups, the Department of Defense under *The Pinkprint* becomes a force for unity rather than division. This is not idealism; it is practical realism, acknowledging that the threats we face are too complex for any one nation to address alone.

Another key aspect of this vision is environmental stewardship. The Department of Defense is one of the largest consumers of fossil fuels in the world, contributing significantly to climate change, a crisis that threatens global security more than any foreign adversary. *The Pinkprint* commits to making the military a leader in sustainability. This means transitioning to renewable energy, reducing waste, and ensuring that defense operations do not exacerbate the very problems they aim to solve. Environmental resilience becomes a core pillar of national security, recognizing that a stable climate is as crucial to safety as any weapon system.

Internally, the Department of Defense itself undergoes a cultural transformation. The military has long been a microcosm of broader societal inequalities, with women, LGBTQ+ individuals, and people of color often facing systemic discrimination. *The Pinkprint* envisions a defense workforce that reflects the diversity of the nation it serves, ensuring that everyone has an equal opportunity to contribute and lead. Training programs emphasize not just tactical skills but empathy, cultural awareness, and conflict resolution. The goal is not just to create better soldiers but better citizens, individuals who see their service as part of a broader commitment to justice and humanity.

Critics may argue that this vision is unrealistic, that the world is too dangerous for anything less than military dominance. But *The Pinkprint* counters that it is precisely this outdated mindset that perpetuates insecurity. A nation armed to the teeth but riddled with inequality and environmental collapse is not secure, it is a powder keg waiting to ignite. Real security comes from addressing the conditions that lead to conflict, not from stockpiling weapons to respond to it. This is a shift from fear to hope, from reaction to prevention, from isolation to interconnectedness.

The Common Defense Fund, as envisioned in *The Pinkprint*, is a model for how the Department of Defense can lead not just in protecting the nation but in redefining what it means to be a global leader. It is a commitment to building a future where safety is not measured by the size of a budget or the reach of a missile but by the health, stability, and prosperity of people at home and around the world. This is the promise of *The Pinkprint*: a defense strategy that defends not just borders but the values and lives that make those borders worth protecting.

Section 2:
The Common Defense Fund
5 Department of Homeland Security (Resilience)
Collective Security & Homeland Solidarity

- A Once Upon a Soon Time Tale

Friends, prepare yourselves; the tale you are about to hear will soften your dreams. "The Common Defense Fund: Department of Homeland Security," in *The Pinkprint* offers a progressive vision for reimagining national security as a system rooted in balance, humanity, and effectiveness. Rather than aggressive enforcement and restrictive policies, this approach prioritizes protecting civil liberties, fostering trust, and strengthening the social fabric of American democracy. Under *The Pinkprint*, security measures are redefined to address the root causes of insecurity, poverty, inequality, and systemic injustice, while maintaining an unwavering commitment to the principles of justice and equity.

National security should not be defined by fear, walls, and hardline enforcement. It should be built on trust, collaboration, and a commitment to human dignity. *The Pinkprint's* vision for the Department of Homeland Resilience rejects the tactics of aggression and exclusion that have too often defined America's approach to security. Instead, it offers a blueprint for a system that prioritizes transparency, accountability, and respect for civil liberties. Security, under this vision, is not about domination or restriction, it is about fostering resilience and unity, both within our borders and beyond them.

The first pillar of this vision is collaboration. Security cannot be achieved by isolated agencies operating behind closed doors, making decisions without input from the communities they claim to protect. Under *The Pinkprint*, national security becomes a partnership, bringing together local governments, civil society organizations, and everyday citizens. Communities, especially those most impacted by past security policies, have a seat at the table in shaping the practices and priorities of the Department of Homeland Resilience. This approach ensures that policies are grounded in lived experience, not abstract theories or political agendas. It recognizes that the people closest to the challenges are also closest to the solutions.

Transparency is the foundation of trust, and trust is the cornerstone of effective security. For too long, national security policies have been cloaked in secrecy, shielding abuses of power from public scrutiny. *The Pinkprint* calls for a radical shift: all security measures must be open to oversight and evaluation. This includes public reporting on enforcement actions, clear accountability structures, and mechanisms for citizens to provide feedback and challenge abuses. Transparency is not a weakness, it is a strength that holds the system accountable and ensures that power is wielded responsibly.

A major focus of this vision is dismantling fear-based strategies that have driven wedges between communities and the government. The policies of surveillance, detention, and exclusion do not make us safer; they breed resentment, distrust, and division. Under *The Pinkprint*, national security policies are reframed to build bridges instead of barriers. Programs that foster dialogue between law enforcement and marginalized communities take precedence, creating environments where safety is a shared goal rather than a contested battle. Enforcement practices are reimagined to prioritize de-escalation and restorative justice, ensuring that security does not come at the expense of human dignity.

Proactive measures are another key element of the Department of Homeland Resilience. Reactive strategies that respond to crises after they occur leave us perpetually on the defensive, fighting fires instead of preventing them. *The Pinkprint* shifts this paradigm by addressing the root causes of insecurity. Investments in education, healthcare, housing, and economic opportunity are central to this approach. By tackling poverty, inequality, and systemic discrimination, the Department strengthens the social fabric that keeps communities safe. A well-educated, healthy, and economically stable society is far less susceptible to the conditions that lead to insecurity.

This vision also recognizes that national security is inherently linked to global security. Borders cannot shield us from the ripple effects of climate change, pandemics, or political instability. The Department of Homeland Resilience, under *The Pinkprint*, takes a holistic approach, working in partnership with international organizations and other nations to address shared challenges. This means participating in global climate agreements, supporting refugees with dignity and compassion, and investing in sustainable development abroad. Security is no longer framed as a zero-sum game where one nation's gain comes at another's loss. Instead, it becomes a collective effort to create a safer, more stable world for everyone.

Respect for civil liberties is non-negotiable in this vision. The surveillance state, with its unchecked expansion over the past two decades, has eroded the very freedoms it claims to protect. *The Pinkprint* demands the dismantling of invasive surveillance programs and the restoration of privacy rights. Security cannot come at the expense of the Constitution. Instead, it must work in harmony with it, ensuring that every citizen's rights are upheld. Whistleblowers who expose abuses are not punished but protected, and independent oversight bodies are empowered to hold the system accountable.

A reimagined Department of Homeland Resilience also requires cultural change within its ranks. Training programs are overhauled to emphasize empathy, cultural competence, and conflict resolution. Law enforcement officers and other security personnel are taught not just how to respond to threats but how to build relationships with the communities they serve. Leadership reflects the diversity of the nation, ensuring that decision-making includes perspectives from every corner of society. This is not about weakening the department but about strengthening it by aligning its values with those of the people it exists to protect.

Finally, this vision recognizes that true security is not just about preventing harm, it is about creating the conditions for people to thrive. Security is not a state of constant vigilance or fear but a sense of confidence in the systems that support us. When communities feel secure in their access to education, healthcare, and opportunity, they are empowered to focus on growth rather than survival. The Department of Homeland Resilience, as envisioned by *The Pinkprint*, becomes a partner in this process, not an enforcer but an enabler of a society where everyone can live with dignity and hope.

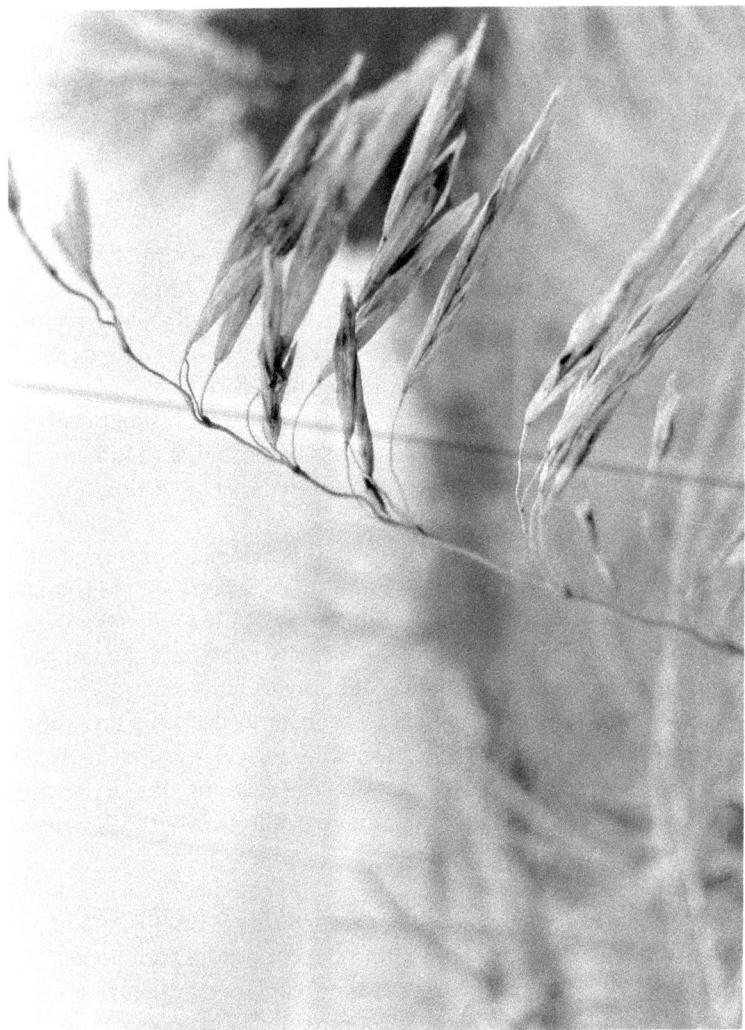

Section 2:
The Common Defense Fund
6 Department of State
The Common Peace Initiative

- A Once Upon a Soon Time Tale

Come closer, for the reassuring account you are about to hear is for the kind-hearted. "The Common Peace Initiative: Department of Global Collaboration," in *The Pinkprint* reimagines America's role in international diplomacy as one of partnership, respect, and shared responsibility. Under *The Pinkprint*, the Department of State becomes a champion of collaborative global efforts, rejecting unilateral action in favor of cooperative problem-solving and mutual benefit. This vision places traditional diplomacy back at the heart of international relations, prioritizing dialogue over confrontation and long-term alliances over transactional deals.

The Pinkprint reimagines the Department of State as a force for global unity, recognizing that the challenges of our time, climate change, pandemics, economic inequality, and human rights abuses, require collective solutions. In a world where borders cannot contain crises, diplomacy becomes the first and most important tool for building a future rooted in equity and sustainability. This vision moves beyond transactional, short-term gains and centers on cooperation, mutual respect, and shared responsibility. America's role in this framework is not to dominate but to lead through collaboration and example, fostering trust and progress in every corner of the globe.

Diplomacy is restored to its rightful place as the cornerstone of foreign policy. The Department of State under *The Pinkprint* becomes a hub for innovation, where nations, organizations, and communities come together to address shared challenges. This vision rejects the confrontational approaches of the past, focusing instead on building lasting relationships. Solutions are not imposed from above but co-created with the voices of those most affected by global challenges. Inclusivity and trust are the guiding principles, ensuring that every decision reflects a commitment to global equity.

Addressing climate change is a central pillar of this approach. The Department leads the charge in international climate negotiations, pushing for agreements that deliver measurable, enforceable results. It champions renewable energy initiatives, offering support to nations transitioning from fossil fuels, and ensures that vulnerable countries have the resources needed to adapt to climate impacts. The goal is not only to reduce emissions but to create a resilient global community capable of withstanding the environmental challenges ahead. This effort recognizes that no nation can tackle climate change alone, and America's leadership lies in fostering a united front against this existential threat.

Global health crises demand similar collaboration. The COVID-19 pandemic exposed the failures of isolationist policies, where nations hoarded resources and vaccines, leaving millions vulnerable. *The Pinkprint* envisions a Department of State that prioritizes equity in global health, advocating for international agreements to ensure vaccines, treatments, and medical supplies are distributed based on need, not wealth. It also invests in strengthening healthcare systems worldwide, recognizing that global health security begins with local resilience. By addressing health disparities, the Department not only protects lives but also reduces the conditions that lead to instability and migration.

Economic inequality is another critical focus. The Department of State promotes fair trade agreements that prioritize workers' rights, environmental sustainability, and economic justice over corporate profits. It supports global efforts to combat corruption and tax evasion, ensuring that resources uplift communities rather than concentrate wealth in the hands of a few. By fostering economic stability and opportunity, the Department helps reduce migration pressures and conflict, creating a foundation for long-term peace and prosperity. This is not charity; it is a recognition that shared prosperity benefits everyone, including America.

Human rights, under *The Pinkprint*, are non-negotiable. The Department leads efforts to hold oppressive fascist regimes accountable, not through military intervention but through coordinated international pressure. Sanctions, diplomatic isolation, and public advocacy are used strategically to protect vulnerable populations and promote democratic values. At the same time,

America confronts its own human rights failings, addressing systemic issues within its borders to lead with credibility and integrity. This dual approach ensures that the values promoted abroad are reflected at home, reinforcing America's role as a global leader in justice and equity.

Technology becomes a powerful tool in this reimagined Department of State. Digital platforms facilitate dialogue between nations, enabling real-time communication and data-driven decision-making. Blockchain ensures transparency in international agreements, while artificial intelligence predicts and mitigates conflicts before they escalate. These innovations enhance diplomacy's effectiveness, making it more responsive and inclusive. Cultural diplomacy is also prioritized, recognizing the power of art, education, and exchange programs to build understanding and goodwill. Programs that bring students, artists, and professionals from different nations together foster connections that endure beyond political cycles, creating a foundation of trust and cooperation.

The reimagined Department of State also emphasizes partnerships with international organizations like the United Nations, World Health Organization, and International Monetary Fund. It works to democratize these institutions, ensuring that smaller and developing nations have a voice in shaping global policies. America's leadership in this space is not about imposing its will but about facilitating collaboration and amplifying the voices of those historically marginalized in global decision-making.

This vision requires a shift in how America views its role on the global stage. Leadership is no longer about asserting dominance or securing unilateral advantages. It is about contributing to a shared future where every nation, community, and individual has the opportunity to thrive. This approach recognizes that America's strength lies not in its ability to control but in its willingness to collaborate. By working together to address shared challenges, nations build a foundation of trust that makes the world safer, more stable, and more equitable.

Section 2:
The Common Defense Fund
7 Intelligence Community
The Common Peace Fund

- A Once Upon a Soon Time Tale

Listen up, folks, because what you are about to learn is deeply
encouraging. "The Common Peace Fund: Intelligence
Community," reimagines America's intelligence apparatus as a
system built on transparency, accountability, and respect for civil
liberties. Rather than prioritizing aggressive intelligence gathering
and operational secrecy, *The Pinkprint* envisions an intelligence
community that safeguards democracy while addressing threats with
precision and ethical integrity. This vision replaces unchecked
power with measured oversight, ensuring that national security does
not come at the expense of individual rights or public trust.

Under this framework, the intelligence community transforms from
an institution defined by secrecy and unchecked power into one
grounded in transparency, accountability, and collaboration. *The
Pinkprint* envisions an intelligence community that safeguards
national security while adhering to the democratic principles of
liberty and justice. Surveillance and secrecy, long its defining
characteristics, give way to openness and trust. The intelligence
community no longer operates as a shadow state but as a
transparent and ethical institution that serves the public interest.

A key shift under this vision is the abandonment of mass
surveillance. For too long, intelligence agencies have relied on broad
and intrusive data collection practices that infringe on civil liberties
and erode trust. Under *The Pinkprint,* these programs are dismantled,
replaced by targeted intelligence gathering based on necessity and
clear oversight. Surveillance becomes a tool of precision rather than
overreach, focusing on specific, verifiable threats. This approach
ensures that the intelligence community enhances security without
compromising the freedoms it exists to protect.

Transparency is a cornerstone of this transformation. Secrecy has
allowed intelligence agencies to act with impunity, shielding abuses
from public scrutiny. *The Pinkprint* reverses this trend by

implementing robust oversight mechanisms. Independent review boards, composed of experts and representatives from civil society, have the authority to evaluate operations, investigate misconduct, and ensure that all activities align with democratic values. Regular public reporting provides transparency while respecting operational security, fostering trust between the intelligence community and the citizens it serves.

Accountability is restored as a fundamental principle. Every action taken by the intelligence community is subject to scrutiny, ensuring that no one operates above the law. Whistleblowers, historically punished for exposing abuses, are protected and recognized as vital safeguards of democracy. Leadership within the intelligence community is held to the highest standards, creating a culture where ethical behavior is not just expected but required. Agencies operate with the understanding that their ultimate accountability is to the people, not to the government or private interests.

Respect for civil liberties becomes a guiding principle in every aspect of intelligence work. Privacy, freedom of expression, and protection from unwarranted intrusion are prioritized at every stage of decision-making. Programs that infringe on these rights, such as warrantless surveillance and bulk data collection, are dismantled. Instead, agencies invest in technologies and practices that enhance privacy while maintaining security. Encryption, anonymized data analysis, and secure communication methods enable intelligence work that respects individual freedoms.

Collaboration replaces isolation as the foundation of the intelligence community's operations. Security is no longer seen as a unilateral effort but as a shared responsibility involving communities, agencies, and international partners. Domestically, intelligence agencies engage directly with the public, building trust through transparency and outreach. They work closely with local organizations to ensure that policies are informed by diverse perspectives and grounded in the realities of the communities they impact. Internationally, the intelligence community fosters alliances based on mutual respect and shared goals, moving away from the exploitative practices of the past.

Technology is leveraged as a force for accountability and precision. Artificial intelligence and machine learning are used to analyze threats efficiently, without infringing on privacy. Blockchain technology creates transparent records of intelligence operations, ensuring that every action can be reviewed and audited. These innovations demonstrate that technology can enhance security while upholding democratic values. By prioritizing ethical and responsible use, the intelligence community becomes a model for how technology can serve the public good.

The intelligence community also embraces a proactive approach to security, focusing on prevention rather than reaction. By addressing the root causes of instability, poverty, inequality, and environmental degradation, it reduces the conditions that lead to conflict and insecurity. Intelligence is used not just to identify threats but to guide policies that mitigate them before they escalate. This shift from a reactive to a preventive mindset enhances global stability and reduces the need for militarized responses.

Training and culture within the intelligence community undergo a profound transformation under *The Pinkprint*. Agents and analysts are equipped not only with technical skills but also with the ethical and cultural competencies needed to navigate a complex, interconnected world. Leadership is intentionally diverse, reflecting the nation's demographics and ensuring decisions are informed by a broad range of perspectives. This cultural shift fosters a workforce that is not only skilled but deeply committed to upholding democracy and human rights, aligning intelligence practices with the values they are meant to protect.

The intelligence community also redefines its global role, prioritizing cooperation over competition and trust over exploitation. Intelligence-sharing agreements are grounded in transparency and mutual respect, fostering stronger alliances and a global culture of accountability. Confronting its history of overreach and secrecy, the intelligence community acknowledges past abuses and commits to reforms that prioritize public accountability and civil liberties. This transformation rebuilds trust, ensuring security is achieved alongside the protection of democratic values, creating a blueprint for a freer, more ethical future.

Section 2:
The Common Defense Fund
8 Media Agencies: U.S. Agency for Global Media
Actual News!

- A Once Upon a Soon Time Tale

Pay close attention, everyone, because this next story is unbelievably exciting. *The Pinkprint* reimagines America's global media strategy, "The Common Defense Fund: Media Agencies U.S. Agency for Global Media," through the lens of transparency, integrity, and the preservation of journalistic independence. The *Common Peace Fund* envisions a media landscape that champions free press principles and balanced reporting while fostering global collaboration and mutual understanding. Instead of ideological conformity and strategic messaging, this vision prioritizes truth, diversity of perspectives, and protects press freedoms at home and abroad.

Under *The Pinkprint*, the U.S. Agency for Global Media (USAGM) transforms into a beacon of ethical journalism and cross-cultural dialogue, reshaping its role from a tool of political influence to a platform for truth and accountability. The reimagined USAGM prioritizes journalistic independence, inclusivity, and transparency, fostering trust between the media, its audience, and the global community. This vision reflects a commitment to preserving democratic principles and ensuring that the media serves as a force for connection and understanding, not manipulation and control.

At the heart of this transformation is the unwavering commitment to journalistic independence. For decades, the media has too often been co-opted as a vehicle for advancing political agendas, eroding public trust and compromising its core mission. *The Pinkprint* rejects this approach entirely, ensuring that all media outlets under the USAGM's purview operate free from governmental or ideological interference. Editorial independence is sacrosanct, with decisions driven by journalistic ethics and public interest rather than political expediency. Leadership within the agency is composed of seasoned journalists and advocates for press freedom, guaranteeing that its operations reflect the values of integrity and fairness.

Transparency becomes a cornerstone of the USAGM's operations, reinforcing its role as a trustworthy source of information. In this new model, accountability is embedded at every level. Regular reporting and oversight mechanisms ensure that editorial decisions and resource allocations are subject to public scrutiny. Mistakes are openly acknowledged and corrected, demonstrating the agency's commitment to accuracy and fostering a culture of accountability. By inviting public engagement and maintaining transparency, the USAGM builds a relationship of trust with its audience, proving that its mission is to inform and empower, not manipulate.

This transformation also emphasizes the power of cross-cultural dialogue. Media is reimagined not as a tool for spreading monolithic narratives but as a space for diverse voices to engage and connect. The USAGM prioritizes stories that highlight shared humanity, explore common struggles, and celebrate cultural richness. This approach moves away from sensationalism and polarization, focusing instead on narratives that inspire empathy and foster mutual understanding. By amplifying marginalized voices and ensuring diverse representation in media production, the agency sets a standard for inclusivity and equity in global storytelling.

Technology is leveraged as a critical enabler of this vision. Digital platforms expand access to reliable information, ensuring that audiences across the globe can engage with credible content free from censorship or bias. The USAGM invests in innovative tools like blockchain to ensure transparency in content distribution and artificial intelligence to combat misinformation. These technologies enhance the agency's ability to uphold journalistic integrity while fostering global conversations that are secure, inclusive, and impactful.

Collaboration becomes a defining characteristic of the reimagined USAGM. Partnerships with international media organizations and grassroots journalism networks replace top-down narratives with a more decentralized and inclusive approach. Training programs and resource-sharing initiatives strengthen media ecosystems worldwide, empowering journalists to operate independently and effectively. These partnerships are built on mutual respect, recognizing that ethical journalism must be locally rooted and globally supported.

The USAGM no longer imposes narratives but facilitates a global dialogue based on shared values of transparency and accountability.

Addressing its legacy of political influence and manipulation is another critical aspect of this transformation. The USAGM openly confronts its past, acknowledging instances where it prioritized ideology over truth. Publicly addressing these failures is a vital step in rebuilding trust. Reparative actions, such as supporting independent journalism in regions where USAGM-backed media once undermined press freedom, demonstrate a genuine commitment to change. This accountability not only strengthens the agency's credibility but also establishes a precedent for ethical reform in global media practices.

Education is a cornerstone of the new USAGM. Media literacy programs empower audiences to critically evaluate information, identify bias, and navigate the digital information landscape. These initiatives cultivate a more informed and discerning public, ensuring that audiences are active participants in democratic processes. By equipping people with the tools to engage thoughtfully with media, the USAGM helps create a culture where truth and accountability are prioritized and protected.

Protecting journalists and media workers is a cornerstone of the USAGM's mission under *The Pinkprint.* In an era where press freedom faces growing threats, the agency stands firm in supporting those who risk their lives to report the truth. By providing legal assistance, resources, and secure platforms, the USAGM ensures persecuted journalists can continue their vital work. This commitment reinforces its role as a defender of free expression and a champion of democratic values, safeguarding the integrity of journalism worldwide.

The reimagined USAGM also redefines media as a public good, prioritizing public interest over profit. By making content accessible to all, regardless of economic or geographic barriers, the agency empowers individuals and communities with knowledge to advocate for themselves and their futures. This vision restores journalism's core principles, truth, accountability, and the common good, positioning the USAGM as a global leader in ethical media practices. It is a blueprint for a freer, more democratic world.

Section 2:
The Common Defense Fund
8 Media Agencies: Corporation for Public Broadcasting
Actual Journalism!

- A Once Upon a Soon Time Tale

Gather 'round, all, for the events you are about to hear are truly realistic. *The Pinkprint* reimagines the Corporation for Public Broadcasting (CPB) as a beacon of journalistic independence, inclusivity, and community engagement. This vision rejects any attempt to reshape public broadcasting into a tool for political agendas, instead emphasizing its role as a vital platform for diverse voices and balanced reporting. The reimagined CPB prioritizes integrity and transparency, ensuring that it serves the public interest rather than ideological conformity.

Under *The Pinkprint*, the Corporation for Public Broadcasting (CPB) transforms into a champion of journalistic independence, cultural enrichment, and community empowerment. It rejects the notion that public broadcasting should serve as a vehicle for political agendas, refocusing on its mission to educate, inform, and connect. This vision elevates the CPB as a vital platform for diverse voices and balanced reporting, ensuring it remains a cornerstone of democracy and a space where truth and inclusivity thrive.

A key pillar of this transformation is the CPB's commitment to representing the full spectrum of American experiences. Public broadcasting becomes a space where marginalized voices and untold stories take center stage, from Indigenous perspectives and immigrant narratives to rural and urban realities. This isn't just about inclusivity for its own sake; it's about fostering empathy and understanding in a divided world. By showcasing the breadth and depth of the American experience, the CPB builds bridges between communities and creates programming that resonates with all.

Editorial independence is a non-negotiable cornerstone of the reimagined CPB. Safeguards are implemented to ensure programming decisions are guided by journalistic integrity and public interest rather than political or ideological pressures.

Leadership within the CPB reflects a commitment to neutrality and expertise, creating a firewall between public broadcasting and outside influences. These measures protect the integrity of public broadcasting and reinforce its role as a trusted source of information and cultural enrichment.

Transparency and accountability are equally critical. The reimagined CPB invites public engagement in its governance and programming, creating opportunities for communities to help shape the content they consume. Public forums, feedback mechanisms, and regular reporting on editorial policies and funding ensure the CPB remains responsive to its audience. This transparency fosters trust, making the CPB a media institution that genuinely reflects and serves the public's needs.

Education is central to the CPB's mission under *The Pinkprint*. Public broadcasting becomes a powerful tool for addressing educational gaps and providing accessible learning opportunities for all. From early childhood programming to adult education initiatives, the CPB invests in content that empowers individuals with knowledge and skills. Partnerships with schools, libraries, and community organizations ensure these resources reach the people who need them most, making public broadcasting a driver of opportunity and lifelong learning.

Cultural programming flourishes under this vision. The CPB becomes a platform where art and storytelling thrive, offering audiences content that entertains, educates, and inspires. From showcasing local traditions to celebrating global artistry, the CPB reinforces its role as a cultural beacon. By supporting independent creators and amplifying diverse artistic voices, public broadcasting nurtures creativity while fostering a deeper appreciation for the shared humanity that art reflects.

Technology plays a transformative role in the reimagined CPB. Digital platforms expand the reach of public broadcasting, ensuring its content is accessible to audiences across geographic and economic divides. Streaming services, interactive learning tools, and mobile applications bring public broadcasting into the digital age, meeting audiences where they are. These innovations enable the

CPB to engage with communities dynamically while maintaining its commitment to the principles of transparency and accountability.

The CPB's role as a champion of journalistic independence extends to global collaborations. In partnership with international public broadcasters, the agency promotes free press principles and supports independent journalism worldwide. By sharing resources and expertise, the CPB helps strengthen media ecosystems in regions where press freedom is under threat. These efforts demonstrate the CPB's commitment to not only informing domestic audiences but also contributing to global progress and accountability.

Addressing its legacy is an essential component of this transformation. The CPB openly acknowledges instances where its programming or practices have fallen short of its mission. By confronting these shortcomings and implementing reparative measures, such as increased funding for underrepresented creators, the CPB demonstrates its dedication to continuous improvement. This accountability rebuilds trust and positions the CPB as a leader in ethical media practices.

Public broadcasting is redefined as a public good rather than a commodity. Content is made accessible to all, free from commercial pressures or profit motives. This ensures the CPB remains focused on serving the public interest, providing content that empowers individuals and communities. The CPB's commitment to transparency, inclusivity, and accountability underscores its role as a media institution that educates and inspires while reinforcing the values of democracy.

Ultimately, *The Pinkprint's* vision for the CPB is about more than transforming public broadcasting, it's about redefining its role in society. The CPB becomes a space where diverse voices are heard, truth is honored, and democracy is strengthened. It fosters a media landscape that connects communities, empowers individuals, and informs the public without bias or manipulation. This reimagined CPB embodies what public media can and should be: a force for good in a world that needs it now more than ever.

Section 2:
The Common Defense Fund
9 Agency for International Development
Ethical Global Development

- A Once Upon a Soon Time Tale

Alright, everyone, hold tight, because what you are about to hear will refresh your senses. *The Pinkprint* reimagines America's approach to international aid and development through a lens of equity, sustainability, and true humanitarianism. "Agency for International Development," prioritizes global cooperation and shared progress over narrow strategic interests and ideological conformity. This vision restores the fundamental goals of international development: alleviating poverty, addressing systemic inequalities, and fostering resilience in communities worldwide. It shifts the focus of aid from being a tool of political leverage to a commitment to mutual respect and collective well-being.

Under *The Pinkprint*, the Agency for Global Development transforms into a model of ethical, transparent, and inclusive international aid, rejecting the transactional nature of traditional development practices. Instead of tying aid to political alignment or strategic interests, the agency prioritizes principles of need, equity, and empowerment. This reimagined approach shifts the focus from control to collaboration, from temporary fixes to sustainable solutions, ensuring that the agency's efforts truly uplift communities and foster lasting change.

Transparency becomes the foundation of this transformation. For too long, international aid has been clouded by opaque decision-making and hidden agendas. *The Pinkprint* demands clarity at every stage, from determining funding priorities to evaluating project outcomes. Aid allocation is guided by clear and publicly available criteria, ensuring that resources are distributed based on urgency and the potential for measurable impact. Regular reporting and accountability mechanisms create a new standard of trust between donors, recipients, and the public. Transparency also extends to the communities served, empowering them with information about how resources are being used and enabling them to hold all stakeholders accountable.

Collaboration replaces the top-down, paternalistic approach that has dominated international development for decades. Programs are no longer imposed from outside but co-created with local leaders, grassroots organizations, and community members. This participatory model ensures that solutions reflect the realities on the ground and that communities have agency in shaping their futures. By involving those most directly affected, the agency builds trust and ensures that its efforts are not only effective but also sustainable. Local ownership becomes a cornerstone of success, with communities actively driving the initiatives that impact their lives.

Inclusion is another critical pillar of *The Pinkprint's* vision. Marginalized groups, such as women, Indigenous peoples, and those living in extreme poverty, are prioritized as key partners in development. These communities, often excluded from decision-making processes despite being disproportionately affected by global challenges, are given a voice at every stage of the process. Their insights and expertise inform the design and implementation of projects, addressing systemic inequities while fostering innovative solutions. By amplifying the voices of the marginalized, the agency not only empowers these groups but also ensures that its programs are equitable and impactful.

Sustainability is at the heart of the reimagined agency's mission. Short-term aid and dependency-inducing practices are replaced with investments in long-term resilience. Renewable energy projects, sustainable agriculture, and climate adaptation programs form the backbone of this approach. Communities are equipped to mitigate the effects of climate change and adapt to environmental challenges, ensuring their stability and prosperity in the face of global crises. Economic empowerment initiatives, such as support for small businesses and fair trade programs, further break cycles of poverty and create self-sustaining systems of growth.

Health and education are integral to this vision. The agency invests in healthcare infrastructure, training medical professionals, and ensuring access to essential medicines and vaccines. These initiatives address immediate health crises while building the capacity for long-term care. Education is equally prioritized, with programs that close literacy gaps, promote gender equity in schooling, and provide vocational training. By empowering individuals with knowledge and skills, the agency fosters stability and opportunity, enabling communities to thrive.

Technology plays a transformative role in *The Pinkprint's* approach. Digital tools streamline aid delivery, ensuring efficiency and transparency while reducing waste. Blockchain technology creates verifiable records of resource allocation, fostering trust and accountability. Mobile platforms improve access to resources for remote and underserved populations, while data analytics enable real-time monitoring and adaptation of programs. Technology enhances not only the efficiency of aid delivery but also the inclusivity of development, ensuring that no community is left behind.

Confronting past failures is an essential component of this transformation. The agency openly acknowledges instances where aid was misused, projects failed, or local autonomy was undermined. Reparative measures, such as increased funding for community-driven initiatives and knowledge-sharing programs, demonstrate a commitment to justice and equity. By learning from its history, the agency rebuilds trust and lays the groundwork for more ethical and impactful development practices moving forward.

Partnerships with international organizations and regional coalitions are redefined to emphasize equity and shared responsibility. The agency collaborates with global allies to address systemic challenges such as climate change, migration, and health crises. These partnerships are built on mutual respect, recognizing that collective action is essential for tackling global problems. The agency's leadership in these efforts positions it as a model for how nations can work together to create a more just and sustainable world.

Ultimately, *The Pinkprint* transforms the Agency for Global Development into a beacon of global solidarity. It rejects exploitation and paternalism in favor of empowerment and partnership. By prioritizing transparency, collaboration, and inclusion, the agency redefines international aid as a commitment to shared progress and resilience. This vision is not just about improving the efficiency of aid, it's about ensuring that development truly serves the people it aims to help.

Section 3:
The General Welfare
10 Department of Agriculture
Real Food, Not Just Corn, Soy, & Subsidies

- A Once Upon a Soon Time Tale

Folks, take a deep breath, because what you are about to hear will leave you in stitches in your britches. Under *The Pinkprint*, the Department of Agriculture (USDA) transforms into a champion of sustainable practices, equitable support, and resilience for farmers, consumers, and the environment. This reimagined vision rejects deregulation and corporate dominance, focusing instead on policies that prioritize small farmers, regenerative agriculture, and food security for all. The USDA becomes a partner to communities rather than an instrument of profit-driven agendas, ensuring that agricultural practices reflect the values of stewardship, sustainability, and shared prosperity.

This framework emphasizes empowering small and family-owned farms as the backbone of American agriculture. Under *The Pinkprint*, the USDA shifts its focus from catering to corporate agribusiness to supporting the independent farmers and local food systems that sustain communities. Accessible funding, technical education, and robust resource networks form the pillars of this transformation. Small farmers no longer face insurmountable barriers to entry or survival; instead, they are equipped with tools to innovate, grow, and thrive. This approach fosters a decentralized agricultural landscape, ensuring that wealth and opportunity are distributed across rural and urban economies alike, reinvigorating local communities while reducing dependence on massive, profit-driven corporations.

The emphasis on small farms also strengthens regional food systems. By supporting local production and distribution, the USDA reduces the need for long supply chains that are vulnerable to disruption and environmental inefficiency. Farmers' markets and community-supported agriculture programs become central to food access, connecting growers directly with consumers. This direct connection not only boosts local economies but also rebuilds trust in the food system. Consumers understand where their food comes from and the values behind its production, creating a stronger bond between farmers and the people they nourish.

Sustainability forms the heart of *The Pinkprint's* vision for agriculture. The USDA invests heavily in regenerative farming practices that rebuild soil health, conserve water, and foster ecological balance. Programs promote crop rotation, cover cropping, and reduced tillage, methods that enhance productivity while safeguarding the environment. Farmers receive incentives to adopt these practices, recognizing that the transition to sustainable methods requires support and shared risk. These investments not only combat soil degradation and water scarcity but also position American agriculture as a global leader in combating climate change. Resilient, adaptive farming systems are no longer a luxury but a necessity for ensuring food security in the face of an uncertain future.

Biodiversity is another critical priority. The USDA actively works to preserve native plant and animal species, recognizing that monocultures and industrial farming practices endanger ecosystems. Programs support pollinator habitats, organic farming, and heirloom seed cultivation, creating a dynamic agricultural system that benefits both the land and the people who depend on it. Additionally, food waste reduction initiatives tackle inefficiencies in the supply chain, ensuring that resources are used wisely and ethically. By addressing waste at every stage, from production to consumption, the USDA under *The Pinkprint* ensures that surplus food benefits communities rather than landfills.

Food security and equity take center stage in *The Pinkprint's* reimagined USDA. Policies prioritize universal access to nutritious, affordable food, with a particular focus on underserved and rural communities often left behind by current systems. Expansion of farmers' markets, mobile food pantries, and local food hubs brings fresh produce to food deserts, ensuring that no community is excluded from the benefits of American agriculture. Nutrition assistance programs are strengthened and modernized, with streamlined access and expanded eligibility to reflect the realities of food insecurity in the modern economy. These measures ensure that agricultural success is not limited to producers but shared with all who rely on their work.

Equity also drives efforts to dismantle systemic barriers that have historically excluded farmers of color, women, and Indigenous communities from agricultural opportunities. *The Pinkprint* calls for targeted grants, mentorship programs, and legal protections to ensure that these groups can thrive within the industry. Restorative initiatives, such as returning land to disenfranchised communities or supporting cooperative farming models, reflect the USDA's commitment to correcting past injustices. This focus on inclusion ensures that American agriculture reflects the diversity of its people and provides opportunities for all.

Technology plays a transformative role in advancing the USDA's mission under *The Pinkprint*. Innovations such as precision agriculture, advanced irrigation systems, and data analytics are made accessible to small and mid-sized farms, democratizing tools that have historically been out of reach. These technologies enable farmers to optimize resources, reduce environmental impact, and increase yields without compromising sustainability. Digital platforms also enhance communication and collaboration within the agricultural community, creating networks where farmers can share knowledge, access markets, and connect with support services.

Global partnerships reinforce the USDA's role as a leader in ethical agricultural practices. By collaborating with international organizations, the USDA supports efforts to address global food insecurity and promote sustainable farming worldwide. These partnerships emphasize knowledge-sharing, capacity-building, and mutual benefit, showcasing American agriculture as a model of innovation and responsibility. By working alongside global allies, the USDA helps tackle challenges such as climate change, migration, and resource scarcity on an international scale.

Finally, *The Pinkprint* emphasizes transparency and accountability in all USDA operations. The department engages directly with farmers, consumers, and advocates to ensure that policies and programs reflect the needs and values of the communities they serve. Public reporting and independent oversight guarantee that the USDA remains responsive and equitable, fostering trust and confidence in its role as a steward of the nation's agricultural future.

Section 3:
The General Welfare
11 Department of Education
Education for All

- A Once Upon a Soon Time Tale

Lean in, friends, because the story you are about to hear will make your skin glow with joy. Under *The Pinkprint*, the Department of Education is reimagined as a champion of equity, inclusivity, and opportunity, prioritizing access to high-quality education for every student, regardless of their background or socioeconomic status. This vision rejects deregulation and the erosion of public education, instead focusing on strengthening public schools as vital community hubs. By emphasizing collaboration, accountability, and investment in underserved communities, *The Pinkprint* ensures that the educational system becomes a force for empowerment and social mobility.

Under *The Pinkprint*, the Department of Education is reimagined as a cornerstone of equity, inclusivity, and opportunity. This vision positions public schools as the heart of their communities, emphasizing their role not just as centers of learning but as engines of empowerment and progress. Rejecting deregulation and privatization, *The Pinkprint* prioritizes strengthening the public education system to ensure every child, regardless of zip code or circumstance, has access to high-quality education. This approach seeks to dismantle systemic barriers, foster social cohesion, and lay the foundation for a more equitable and just society.

At the heart of this transformation is a commitment to equity. *The Pinkprint* recognizes that public education has long mirrored and perpetuated societal inequalities, and it boldly addresses these disparities by directing resources where they are most needed. Schools in underserved areas receive increased funding to improve facilities, provide advanced technology, and attract and retain high-quality educators. Investments in transportation, nutrition programs, and after-school initiatives ensure that students in low-income communities have the same opportunities to succeed as their more privileged peers. Equity isn't just a principle; it is the guiding force behind every policy, with the understanding that closing opportunity gaps benefits everyone.

Public education is elevated as a shared societal good, an essential pillar of democracy. *The Pinkprint* rejects the diversion of public funds to privatized school choice programs, which too often exacerbate inequities and siphon resources from already underfunded public schools. Instead, it champions the idea that diverse, inclusive classrooms strengthen communities and prepare students to thrive in a multicultural world. Schools become places where students of all backgrounds learn together, breaking down the divisions that too often separate people in society. This collaborative environment fosters empathy, critical thinking, and civic responsibility, skills essential for building a cohesive and democratic nation.

Teachers are the backbone of this vision. Recognizing the vital role educators play, *The Pinkprint* calls for significant investments in teacher salaries, benefits, and professional development. It also prioritizes recruitment and retention programs to build a diverse teaching workforce that reflects the demographics of the student population. By empowering teachers with the resources and autonomy they need to succeed, this approach ensures that classrooms are places of innovation and inspiration. Educators are no longer seen as mere deliverers of curriculum but as mentors and leaders who shape the next generation.

Accountability is redefined under *The Pinkprint* to reflect a broader understanding of student success. Standardized tests, while a useful tool, are no longer the sole measure of a school's performance. Instead, assessments are holistic, valuing creativity, problem-solving, and socio-emotional growth alongside academic achievement. Schools are held accountable for creating environments where all students can thrive, with transparency and community involvement central to the process. Families, educators, and local leaders have a seat at the table, ensuring that policies reflect the needs and aspirations of the communities they serve.

Community schools emerge as a transformative model in *The Pinkprint's* vision. These schools go beyond academics, serving as hubs for health care, mental health services, and family support. By addressing the broader social and economic challenges that impact learning, community schools create conditions where students can fully engage in their education. Partnerships with local organizations and businesses enhance these efforts, ensuring that resources are tailored to meet the unique needs of each community. This integrated approach recognizes that education does not happen in isolation, it is deeply connected to the well-being of families and neighborhoods.

Higher education is also a key focus of this reimagined Department of Education. Access to college and vocational training is no longer a privilege reserved for the wealthy but a right for all who wish to pursue it. *The Pinkprint* invests in reducing tuition costs, expanding financial aid, and supporting community colleges as gateways to opportunity. Apprenticeships and job training programs are prioritized to prepare students for meaningful careers in a rapidly evolving economy. By removing financial barriers and expanding pathways to success, the Department ensures that higher education becomes a tool for social mobility rather than a driver of inequality.

Technology is thoughtfully harnessed under *The Pinkprint* to expand access and enhance learning without exacerbating disparities. Digital tools and online platforms complement traditional instruction, particularly in rural and underserved areas, ensuring every student has access to modern educational resources. Schools are equipped with the necessary infrastructure to fully integrate these advancements, while safeguards prevent the commercialization of education. Technology is not used to widen the gap but to bridge it, serving the needs of students and educators rather than corporate interests.

Curriculum reforms ensure education reflects the diversity and complexity of the world students will inherit. Inclusive histories and cultural understanding are prioritized, fostering empathy and global awareness. Anti-bias programs create safe, supportive environments where every student feels valued and empowered. Ultimately, *The Pinkprint* redefines the Department of Education as a champion of equity and inclusivity, transforming schools into vital community hubs that empower students to thrive and contribute to a fairer, more united society.

Section 3:
The General Welfare
12 Department Energy and Related Commissions
Publicly Owned Utilities

- A Once Upon a Soon Time Tale

Listen carefully, everyone, because the tale you are about to hear is utterly enlightening. Under *The Pinkprint*, the Department of Energy (DOE) is reimagined as a champion of sustainable energy, environmental stewardship, and public ownership of critical utilities. This vision rejects the prioritization of corporate profits and deregulation in favor of policies that serve the public interest and address the urgent need for climate resilience. The reimagined DOE places sustainability, equity, and innovation at the forefront, ensuring that energy policies align with long-term environmental protection and community empowerment.

Central to *The Pinkprint's* reimagining of the Department of Energy is the principle of public ownership, a transformative shift that places energy resources directly under community control. For decades, private interests have dictated energy policy, prioritizing profit margins over equitable access and environmental stewardship. Under this new framework, energy utilities are publicly owned and operated, ensuring that decisions are driven by the needs of people and communities, not shareholders. Public ownership prioritizes affordability and reliability, establishing a system where energy is treated as a fundamental right rather than a commodity. Communities gain control of critical infrastructure, enabling them to direct investments into renewable projects, modernize outdated grids, and build resilience against increasingly severe climate impacts. This model fosters accountability and ensures that energy systems serve the greater good, addressing inequities that have long plagued rural and underserved areas.

Sustainability is not an afterthought; it is the cornerstone of *The Pinkprint's* vision for the Department of Energy. Fossil fuels, which have long dominated American energy policy, are phased out in favor of renewable sources such as solar, wind, and geothermal. Massive investments in clean energy infrastructure drive this transition, supporting the rapid deployment of renewable projects while creating thousands of well-paying jobs in a sector poised for growth. Programs incentivize clean energy adoption, making it accessible for households, businesses, and municipalities. Simultaneously, funding is allocated for cutting-edge research into technologies like energy storage, hydrogen fuel cells, and advanced grid systems. These innovations enhance efficiency and ensure that renewable energy is not only sustainable but also reliable enough to meet the demands of modern society. This commitment to renewables positions the United States as a global leader in combating climate change while securing its energy independence.

Equity forms the backbone of every energy policy under *The Pinkprint*. Rural areas and historically underserved communities, which have often been the last to benefit from energy advancements, are placed at the forefront of this transformation. Infrastructure projects prioritize closing gaps in access to affordable, reliable energy in these regions, ensuring no one is left behind in the transition to a cleaner, greener energy system. Community-based initiatives empower local leaders to spearhead projects tailored to their unique needs, fostering economic development and energy independence at the grassroots level. Microgrids, community solar farms, and localized energy storage solutions provide resilience and autonomy to areas previously dependent on distant, profit-driven utilities. This decentralized approach strengthens communities, ensuring that the benefits of the energy transition are shared equitably.

Transparency and accountability are woven into the fabric of this reimagined DOE. Decision-making processes are democratized, inviting input from a broad range of stakeholders, including scientists, environmental advocates, and community members. Public forums, advisory committees, and regular reporting on energy policies and environmental impacts foster trust and ensure that the department operates with integrity. Energy policies are no longer crafted behind closed doors; they are shaped in collaboration with the very people they affect. This openness not only strengthens public confidence but also ensures that the DOE remains aligned with evolving societal values and environmental imperatives.

Public ownership and sustainability are not mutually exclusive; they are complementary goals that redefine how energy systems function.

Under *The Pinkprint*, publicly owned utilities invest heavily in renewable infrastructure while maintaining a commitment to affordability and reliability. Energy revenues, which once enriched private shareholders, are reinvested into the system to fund advancements, support low-income households, and prepare for future challenges. This model creates a self-sustaining cycle of improvement and innovation, where the focus remains firmly on public benefit rather than corporate profit.

Technology plays a critical role in advancing this vision. Smart grids and advanced energy storage systems enable efficient management of renewable resources, reducing waste and enhancing reliability. Investments in research and development drive breakthroughs that make clean energy more accessible and affordable. Digital tools and platforms improve transparency, allowing consumers to track energy usage and costs while contributing to grid stability. These technological advancements demonstrate that public ownership and cutting-edge innovation can coexist, creating an energy system that is not only modern but also deeply aligned with the principles of equity and sustainability.

Addressing the legacy of environmental harm caused by fossil fuels is central to *The Pinkprint*. The DOE prioritizes cleanup programs for abandoned mines, oil wells, and contaminated sites, restoring ecosystems and public spaces while rebuilding trust in government stewardship. By focusing on environmental justice, these efforts ensure that communities most affected by pollution are first to benefit from the transition to renewable energy.

This transformation drives economic resilience through public investment in the renewable energy sector, creating stable, high-quality jobs. Training programs and apprenticeships help fossil fuel workers transition to roles in clean energy, fostering long-term stability. Energy becomes a public good, accessible to all and managed for future generations. By prioritizing equity, sustainability, and community empowerment, *The Pinkprint* redefines energy systems and sets a new standard for leadership rooted in integrity and purpose.

Section 3:
The General Welfare
13 Environmental Protection Agency
Fair Environmental Stewardship

- A Once Upon a Soon Time Tale

Gather around, because the events you are about to hear about will make the hairs on your arm stand up and salute, in relief that we are finally going to address the climate crisis. Under *The Pinkprint,* the Environmental Protection Agency (EPA) is reimagined as a true guardian of environmental health and public well-being. This vision rejects deregulation and unchecked industry collaboration in favor of policies that prioritize environmental protection, climate resilience, and equitable health outcomes. Instead of serving industrial interests, the reimagined EPA becomes a champion of sustainability, enforcing robust safeguards and ensuring that the planet and its people are protected for generations to come.

Under *The Pinkprint,* the Environmental Protection Agency (EPA) is reimagined as a steadfast protector of the planet and public health. This vision turns away from prioritizing corporate profits and deregulation and focuses on bold, actionable policies that safeguard natural resources, combat climate change, and ensure clean air and water for all. The reimagined EPA becomes a true ally to communities, enforcing environmental laws with integrity and empowering local efforts to create a healthier, more sustainable future.

At the heart of this transformation is a commitment to robust environmental safeguards. No longer beholden to industrial interests, the EPA under *The Pinkprint* enforces strict regulations on pollution and emissions. Clean air and water are not negotiable privileges but basic rights that the agency protects with unwavering resolve. Industries are held accountable for their environmental impacts, and those that fail to meet standards are subject to meaningful penalties. This strict enforcement ensures that environmental protection is no longer a backseat consideration but a driving force in policy and practice.

Climate resilience takes center stage in the reimagined EPA. As the impacts of climate change become more pronounced, the agency prioritizes strategies to mitigate its effects and adapt to its challenges. Investments are funneled into renewable energy infrastructure, wetland restoration, reforestation projects, and urban greening initiatives. These efforts combat rising temperatures, reduce flooding risks, and enhance biodiversity, creating natural buffers against environmental disasters. Community-based climate programs empower local leaders to develop solutions tailored to their unique challenges, ensuring resilience is built from the ground up.

Equity underpins every action the EPA takes under *The Pinkprint*. Historically, low-income communities and communities of color have borne the brunt of environmental degradation, from polluted water sources to industrial waste sites. The EPA commits to rectifying these injustices by prioritizing environmental justice initiatives. Resources are directed to clean up toxic sites, improve air quality, and monitor industrial activity in these vulnerable areas. Residents are given a seat at the table in decision-making processes, ensuring their voices shape the policies that directly affect their lives. This focus on fairness not only addresses past harm but also ensures a future where environmental protections benefit everyone equally.

Transparency becomes a defining feature of the EPA's operations. Under *The Pinkprint*, the agency opens its decision-making processes to public scrutiny, inviting input from scientists, environmental advocates, and everyday citizens. Regular reporting on environmental conditions and policy outcomes fosters trust and ensures accountability. This openness strengthens the EPA's role as a trusted guardian of public health and the environment, restoring public confidence that may have eroded in years past.

Technology is leveraged as a powerful tool to advance the EPA's mission. Real-time monitoring systems track air and water quality, enabling swift responses to environmental threats. Advanced modeling tools predict climate impacts and guide proactive policies. Publicly accessible data platforms empower communities to understand local environmental conditions and advocate for necessary changes. These technological advancements not only enhance the EPA's efficiency but also ensure that its work is rooted in the best available science.

Education and community engagement play pivotal roles in this transformation. The reimagined EPA works hand-in-hand with schools, nonprofits, and local governments to promote environmental literacy and foster a culture of stewardship. Programs teach citizens how to reduce waste, conserve water, and advocate for cleaner neighborhoods. These initiatives empower individuals to take ownership of their local environments, creating a collective movement toward sustainability.

Addressing past failures is a key priority for the reimagined EPA. The agency openly acknowledges instances where its enforcement has fallen short or where communities were left vulnerable to environmental harm. Reparative actions, such as expedited cleanups of hazardous sites and investments in community health programs, demonstrate a commitment to justice and rebuilding trust. By confronting its history with humility and resolve, the EPA lays the groundwork for a stronger, more accountable future.

Economic growth and environmental protection are no longer seen as mutually exclusive. The EPA fosters innovation in green industries, creating jobs in renewable energy, sustainable agriculture, and eco-friendly manufacturing. Businesses that prioritize sustainability are supported through grants, tax incentives, and streamlined permitting processes. This approach proves that a thriving economy can coexist with a thriving planet, benefiting both people and the environment.

Ultimately, *The Pinkprint* transforms the EPA into a model of what environmental governance should be: fair, transparent, and focused on the well-being of all. By prioritizing sustainability, justice, and community empowerment, the reimagined EPA sets a new standard for how governments can protect their citizens and the natural world. It moves beyond rhetoric to action, ensuring that the environment is not just preserved but restored, nurtured, and celebrated for generations to come.

Section 3:
The General Welfare
14 Department of Health and Human Services

- A Once Upon a Soon Time Tale

Folks, prepare yourselves for what is about to be revealed; it's nothing short of revelatory and sane. "The General Welfare: Department of Health & Human Services (HHS)," in *The Pinkprint*, is reimagined as a cornerstone of equity, access, and community-centered care. This vision rejects deregulation and ideological agendas, focusing instead on comprehensive healthcare access, robust public health protections, and the well-being of all people, particularly vulnerable populations. The reimagined HHS prioritizes inclusivity, innovation, and accountability, ensuring that healthcare and human services are universally accessible and rooted in compassion rather than partisanship.

This transformation begins with a profound commitment to healthcare equity, addressing the systemic barriers that have long excluded marginalized communities from accessing the care they need. Under *The Pinkprint*, the Department of Health and Human Services (HHS) expands Medicaid, fortifies protections for individuals with pre-existing conditions, and invests heavily in underserved areas. These actions are not stopgaps, they are the foundation of a system designed to place people at the center of policy decisions, ensuring healthcare is universally accessible and tailored to meet the unique needs of every community. Mobile health units and telehealth services become lifelines for rural and remote populations, while urban centers benefit from expanded community clinics offering comprehensive, low-cost care. This approach dismantles the profit-driven healthcare paradigm, replacing it with one that prioritizes compassion, inclusivity, and the fundamental right to health.

Public health protections under *The Pinkprint* are not just preserved; they are elevated to unprecedented levels. The HHS evolves into a leader in tackling the nation's most urgent health challenges, from managing pandemics to addressing the opioid epidemic and widespread mental health crises. Science-based policies guide every decision, with an emphasis on prevention, early intervention, and innovative treatment programs. Funding is directed toward groundbreaking research on emerging diseases, community-based initiatives to combat addiction, and nationwide campaigns to reduce stigma around mental health care. Collaboration becomes the cornerstone of public health strategy, with the HHS forging partnerships at the local, national, and global levels to ensure responses are comprehensive, inclusive, and proactive. Public health is no longer treated as an emergency response system but as a continuous investment in the resilience and well-being of every individual.

Recognizing that health outcomes are deeply influenced by social determinants, the HHS adopts a holistic approach to healthcare delivery. The interconnectedness of housing, education, employment, and nutrition is integrated into health strategies, ensuring that every individual has access to the building blocks of a healthy life. Initiatives to combat food insecurity expand access to fresh, nutritious meals through school programs, community gardens, and mobile food pantries. Affordable childcare and workforce training programs empower families to achieve economic stability, which in turn improves their access to healthcare and other critical services. These efforts acknowledge that health is more than the absence of illness, it is about creating a world where dignity, opportunity, and stability are within everyone's reach.

In *The Pinkprint's* vision, the HHS becomes an engine for systemic reform, rejecting partisan influences and ideologically driven policies that have often undermined public health goals. Inclusivity becomes the defining principle of the department's operations. Health policies are co-created with input from communities, healthcare providers, and advocacy groups, ensuring they reflect the diverse realities of the populations they serve. Programs are tailored to meet the unique needs of LGBTQ+ individuals, people with disabilities, and other historically marginalized groups, addressing gaps in care and fostering an environment of trust and respect. Equity is not treated as an afterthought but as the primary driver of every decision, guaranteeing that the most vulnerable are prioritized at every stage of policy implementation.

The HHS under *The Pinkprint* also redefines the role of healthcare workers, recognizing them as essential partners in achieving health equity. Investments in training, fair wages, and workplace protections ensure that doctors, nurses, and caregivers are supported and valued. Loan forgiveness programs and scholarships are expanded to encourage diverse individuals to pursue careers in healthcare, ensuring that the workforce reflects the communities it serves. These measures create a sustainable pipeline of skilled professionals who are empowered to deliver high-quality, culturally competent care.

Technology plays a transformative role in realizing *The Pinkprint's* vision for HHS. Digital health platforms expand access to care, enabling patients to connect with providers regardless of location. Data analytics are used to identify health disparities and target interventions effectively, ensuring resources are deployed where they are needed most. Telemedicine becomes a standard feature of healthcare delivery, breaking down geographic and logistical barriers to access. These advancements are accompanied by strict privacy protections, ensuring that technological innovation enhances trust rather than eroding it.

Addressing the failures of the past is a central tenet of *The Pinkprint*. The HHS openly confronts the systemic inequities and neglect that have harmed vulnerable populations, implementing reparative actions to rebuild trust. Initiatives to close the maternal health gap, reduce racial disparities in health outcomes, and improve care for Indigenous communities demonstrate a commitment to justice and accountability. These efforts are not merely symbolic; they are tangible steps toward creating a healthcare system that lives up to its promise of serving everyone equally.

Economic benefits flow naturally from this transformation. By investing in preventive care and addressing social determinants of health, the HHS reduces the financial burden of chronic diseases and emergency interventions. A healthier population translates into a more productive workforce, while job creation in community clinics, mental health services, and public health initiatives strengthens local economies. This virtuous cycle reinforces the idea that a robust healthcare system is not only a moral imperative but also a cornerstone of a thriving society.

Section 3:
The General Welfare
15 Department of Housing and Urban Development
Fair Housing is Dignity

- A Once Upon a Soon Time Tale

Everyone, brace yourselves for the uplifting story you are about to hear. Under *The Pinkprint,* the Department of Housing and Urban Development (HUD) is reimagined as a driving force for equity, inclusivity, and sustainable community development. This vision rejects deregulation and profit-driven approaches, focusing instead on ensuring safe, affordable housing as a fundamental right for all. HUD's policies prioritize investments in public housing, tenant protections, and community-led development initiatives that uplift marginalized populations and combat systemic inequalities. By addressing housing as a cornerstone of economic and social stability, *The Pinkprint* transforms HUD into a champion of opportunity.

This reimagined HUD, under *The Pinkprint,* becomes a transformative force for addressing housing inequality and fostering vibrant, inclusive communities. Central to this vision is the principle that housing is a fundamental right, not a commodity to be exploited. To achieve this, HUD prioritizes targeted investments in public housing and mixed-income developments that meet the needs of diverse communities. These projects focus on creating not just shelter but thriving neighborhoods with access to quality schools, transportation, and green spaces. By integrating affordable housing into urban, suburban, and rural landscapes, HUD ensures that housing equity is not confined to isolated pockets but spread across regions, breaking down the divides that have long defined American housing policy.

Rent control measures and strengthened tenant protections form a cornerstone of *The Pinkprint's* approach. With rising rents driving many families into instability or homelessness, HUD enforces policies to cap rent increases, prevent unjust evictions, and hold landlords accountable for maintaining safe, livable housing. These measures provide immediate relief to renters while fostering a housing market that prioritizes stability over speculative profit. At the same time, HUD works to expand and modernize housing assistance programs like Section 8, making them more accessible to those in need. These updates include streamlining application processes, increasing voucher values to reflect local markets, and ensuring portability so families can choose homes in areas with better opportunities.

Tackling homelessness is a central mission of the reimagined HUD. *The Pinkprint* shifts the department's focus from temporary shelters to permanent housing solutions, adopting a "housing first" philosophy that recognizes stable housing as the foundation for addressing other challenges. Comprehensive support systems integrate housing with wraparound services like job training, healthcare, mental health care, and substance abuse treatment. This holistic approach not only provides immediate relief but also addresses the root causes of homelessness, empowering individuals and families to rebuild their lives. Special emphasis is placed on supporting vulnerable populations, including veterans, youth aging out of foster care, and survivors of domestic violence, ensuring that no one is left behind.

Community-led development is a key pillar of *The Pinkprint's* vision for HUD. Decision-making processes are democratized, giving residents and local leaders a voice in shaping the policies and projects that impact their neighborhoods. From participatory budgeting to public forums, these initiatives ensure that housing solutions reflect the unique needs and aspirations of each community. HUD also partners with nonprofit organizations, cooperatives, and community land trusts to expand innovative housing models that prioritize long-term affordability and local control.

Environmental sustainability is integrated into every aspect of housing policy under *The Pinkprint* HUD invests in energy-efficient building designs, renewable energy systems, and sustainable infrastructure to reduce environmental impact and lower utility costs for residents. Programs also focus on retrofitting existing housing stock to meet modern energy and safety standards, ensuring that older buildings remain viable and affordable options. Green building initiatives prioritize the health and well-being of residents, incorporating features like improved ventilation, non-toxic materials, and access to outdoor spaces. These efforts align housing policy with broader climate goals while creating healthier, more livable communities.

HUD's role extends beyond providing shelter; it works to address the systemic issues that create and perpetuate housing insecurity. Recognizing the interconnectedness of housing with education, employment, and health, the department adopts a holistic approach to community development. Programs to combat food deserts, expand public transportation, and provide workforce development opportunities ensure that residents have access to the resources they need to thrive. This comprehensive strategy acknowledges that stable housing is only one piece of the puzzle and works to build communities where opportunity is within reach for all.

Transparency and accountability are central to *The Pinkprint's* reimagined HUD. The department operates with open decision-making processes, regularly reporting on housing initiatives and their outcomes. Public engagement is encouraged at every step, ensuring that policies are informed by the people they affect. This commitment to transparency builds trust and ensures that HUD remains focused on its mission of serving the public good. Data-driven analysis and community feedback guide continuous improvement, making HUD a model of responsive and responsible governance.

Economic empowerment is a natural outcome of *The Pinkprint's* approach to housing. By creating stable, affordable housing and investing in local infrastructure, HUD stimulates economic growth and revitalizes communities. Construction and renovation projects generate jobs, while improved housing stability enables residents to focus on education, employment, and personal growth. These ripple effects demonstrate that equitable housing policy is not just a social imperative but also a driver of broader economic resilience.

Ultimately, *The Pinkprint* transforms HUD into a champion of dignity and opportunity. By prioritizing affordability, sustainability, and community empowerment, the reimagined department ensures that housing policies reflect the values of fairness and inclusion. It moves beyond the idea of housing as a market commodity to embrace it as a public good, essential for the well-being of individuals and society.

Section 3:
The General Welfare
16 Department of the Interior
Beginning Amends and Respect

- A Once Upon a Soon Time Tale

Gather around, because the events you are about to hear about are truly overdue and welcome. "The General Welfare: Department of the Interior," is reimagined in *The Pinkprint* as a steadfast steward of America's natural resources and public lands, prioritizing conservation, community empowerment, and environmental justice over corporate interests and exploitation. This vision rejects deregulation and unchecked resource extraction, focusing instead on sustainable practices that preserve the nation's natural heritage for future generations. Public lands are no longer viewed as commodities to be exploited but as shared treasures to be protected, restored, and enjoyed by all.

Central to the transformation of the Department of the Interior under *The Pinkprint* is a commitment to Indigenous sovereignty and environmental justice. This vision begins with a long-overdue recognition of the historical injustices inflicted upon Indigenous tribes and the urgent need to restore their rightful stewardship of the lands they have protected for centuries. The Department works in partnership with tribal governments to return land rights and decision-making authority to Indigenous communities, ensuring their sovereignty is not merely acknowledged but actively supported. This includes restoring access to sacred sites, expanding co-management agreements, and providing resources for sustainable development initiatives led by tribes. This shift is not just reparative, it lays the foundation for a more just and sustainable approach to land management that benefits all.

Traditional ecological knowledge becomes a cornerstone of the Department's new approach. Indigenous practices, which have long prioritized harmony with the land, offer invaluable insights into sustainable resource management. By integrating these practices into broader policies, the Department fosters land use strategies that prioritize conservation, biodiversity, and resilience. For example, controlled burns, water management techniques, and habitat restoration methods used by tribes are adopted on a larger scale, ensuring that public lands are not only preserved but also restored to their natural health. This partnership exemplifies how Indigenous leadership can guide the nation toward a more sustainable and equitable future.

Environmental justice takes center stage alongside Indigenous sovereignty. For too long, the burden of environmental degradation has fallen disproportionately on low-income communities and communities of color, many of which are situated near resource extraction sites or industrial facilities. Under *The Pinkprint*, the Department launches targeted initiatives to address these inequities, focusing on cleaning up contaminated lands, improving air and water quality, and holding polluters accountable. These efforts prioritize communities that have been neglected for decades, ensuring that all Americans, regardless of socioeconomic status, benefit from clean, healthy environments. The Department's work extends beyond remediation, with proactive measures to prevent future harm and promote environmental equity across all regions.

Conservation becomes the backbone of the Department's mission. Public lands, often seen as assets for industrial use, are redefined as treasures to be protected and enjoyed by all. National parks, wildlife refuges, and wilderness areas are expanded and revitalized, with investments in habitat restoration, reforestation, and climate adaptation projects. Renewable energy development takes precedence over resource extraction, with solar, wind, and geothermal projects carefully planned to minimize environmental impact. The Department implements strict environmental safeguards to ensure that any development on public lands aligns with long-term conservation goals. This focus on protecting natural resources ensures that future generations inherit a landscape that reflects the nation's values of stewardship and sustainability.

Community-led initiatives become a cornerstone of land management practices. The Department democratizes decision-making, inviting input from local communities, environmental organizations, and scientific experts. Public forums, citizen advisory boards, and collaborative planning sessions ensure that policies reflect the needs and values of the people most directly affected. Community land trusts and cooperatives are supported to give residents greater control over local resources, fostering a sense of ownership and responsibility. These partnerships enhance trust between the Department and the public, creating a model of governance that is inclusive, transparent, and responsive.

Economic resilience emerges as a natural outcome of this transformation. The Department invests in sustainable industries such as eco-tourism, renewable energy, and land restoration, creating jobs that align with conservation goals. Workers from extractive industries are provided with training and support to transition into these emerging fields, ensuring that economic opportunities are not sacrificed in the pursuit of environmental protection. This approach proves that environmental stewardship and economic prosperity are not mutually exclusive but mutually reinforcing.

Technology plays a transformative role in advancing the Department's mission. Advanced mapping and monitoring systems enable real-time tracking of land use, ensuring compliance with environmental regulations and preventing illegal activities like poaching and logging. Publicly accessible data platforms empower communities to monitor environmental conditions and advocate for changes when needed. Innovations in renewable energy and sustainable agriculture are integrated into land management actions.

Addressing the impacts of climate change is another central priority. Coastal restoration projects combat erosion and protect vulnerable ecosystems, while water conservation initiatives address droughts and resource scarcity. Reforestation programs and carbon sequestration projects contribute to global climate goals while enhancing the health of public lands. These efforts recognize that the Department's role is not limited to preserving the environment, it also includes preparing for and mitigating the challenges posed by a rapidly changing climate.

This transformation ensures that public lands and natural resources serve the collective good, protecting the planet while empowering the people who depend on it. By prioritizing conservation, equity, and sustainability, the Department sets a new standard for what responsible and inclusive land management can achieve.

Section 3:
The General Welfare
17 Department of Justice
Scales that are Truly Blind

- A Once Upon a Soon Time Tale

Friends, hold on tight; the tale you are about to hear is absolutely fair and balanced, for real. "The General Welfare: Department of Justice (DOJ)," is reimagined in *The Pinkprint* as a defender of civil rights, equity, and justice for all. This transformation rejects the punitive, ideological approach of aggressive enforcement and deregulation, focusing instead on restoring trust in the justice system, protecting vulnerable populations, and addressing systemic inequities. The reimagined DOJ prioritizes accountability, transparency, and the rule of law, ensuring that its mission aligns with the principles of fairness and compassion, rather than serving partisan agendas.

Under *The Pinkprint,* the Department of Justice (DOJ) becomes a beacon of fairness, equity, and accountability, committed to safeguarding civil rights, advancing social justice, and holding all individuals accountable under the law. This reimagined DOJ recognizes that justice must be applied without bias or privilege, ensuring that no one is above the law and no one is left behind. By tackling systemic injustices, addressing abuses of power, and enforcing transparency, *The Pinkprint* creates a justice system that reflects the values of equity, inclusivity, and accountability.

Central to this vision is a commitment to dismantling systemic inequities that disproportionately harm marginalized communities. The DOJ actively enforces civil rights laws, combating discrimination in housing, employment, education, and beyond. Investigations into patterns of racial profiling and police misconduct are prioritized, with reforms targeting the root causes of these injustices. Protections for LGBTQ+ individuals, people with disabilities, and other historically disenfranchised groups are strengthened, ensuring that everyone, regardless of their identity or background, has equal access to justice and opportunity.

A transformative pillar of *The Pinkprint* is the abolition of private prisons. The DOJ ends the federal use of for-profit detention facilities, recognizing that incarcerating individuals for profit undermines the integrity of the justice system. Resources are redirected toward rehabilitation programs, restorative justice initiatives, and alternatives to incarceration that focus on addressing the root causes of crime. The elimination of private prisons also paves the way for broader reforms, including reducing prison populations and addressing racial disparities in sentencing. These changes signal a commitment to a justice system that values humanity over profit.

Mass incarceration is tackled head-on, with sweeping reforms to sentencing laws and practices. Mandatory minimum sentences, which have disproportionately affected communities of color, are abolished. The DOJ advocates for fairer sentencing guidelines and implements programs to help individuals reintegrate into society, reducing recidivism and fostering community stability. Juvenile justice reforms prioritize rehabilitation over punishment, recognizing the importance of supporting young people to reach their potential. By focusing on rehabilitation rather than punishment, *The Pinkprint* ensures that the justice system contributes to public safety and individual opportunity.

Accountability is a non-negotiable principle under *The Pinkprint*. The DOJ ensures that no one is above the law, from private citizens to public officials. Investigations into abuses of power, corruption, and attempts to undermine democracy are pursued rigorously. This includes holding accountable those involved in coup attempts, whether they are rioters, members of Congress, or even a former president. By applying the law evenly and transparently, the DOJ restores public trust and reinforces the rule of law as the foundation of democracy.

The DOJ also becomes a fierce defender of voting rights. It challenges discriminatory redistricting efforts, combats voter suppression, and ensures access to polling places, particularly in underserved communities. Protecting the right to vote is seen not as a partisan issue but as a cornerstone of a functioning democracy. The department works closely with local governments and advocacy groups to ensure that every citizen can participate freely and fairly in elections, safeguarding the integrity of the democratic process.

Transparency and public trust are woven into every aspect of *The Pinkprint's* reimagined DOJ. The department commits to open communication, regularly updating the public on its priorities and progress. Independent oversight mechanisms are established to ensure accountability within the DOJ itself, creating a system of checks and balances that fosters trust. By prioritizing transparency, the DOJ demonstrates its dedication to serving the people, not partisan or corporate interests.

Under *The Pinkprint*, the DOJ reimagines its relationship with communities by prioritizing trust, transparency, and collaboration. Community policing becomes the cornerstone of its approach, shifting from militarized enforcement to neighborhood-focused support. Officers are trained in de-escalation, cultural awareness, and trauma-informed care, fostering partnerships rather than perpetuating fear. Independent oversight bodies investigate allegations of misconduct, ensuring accountability and rebuilding public trust in law enforcement. By emphasizing transparency and community engagement, the DOJ aims to create a justice system that reflects fairness and mutual respect.

Restorative justice initiatives take center stage in the DOJ's reform strategy, focusing on addressing harm while fostering reconciliation and healing. Programs that unite offenders, victims, and community members aim to repair relationships and create opportunities for redemption. Juvenile justice reforms emphasize intervention and support, steering young people away from the criminal justice system and toward positive, productive futures. These initiatives move the DOJ away from punitive practices, instead prioritizing solutions that build stronger, more resilient communities.

The *Pinkprint* DOJ also tackles the root causes of crime through targeted investments in prevention and community development. Resources are directed toward addressing poverty, housing instability, and education gaps that contribute to cycles of incarceration. By integrating restorative practices with community-driven solutions, the DOJ creates a justice system that not only enforces laws but actively works to dismantle systemic inequities.

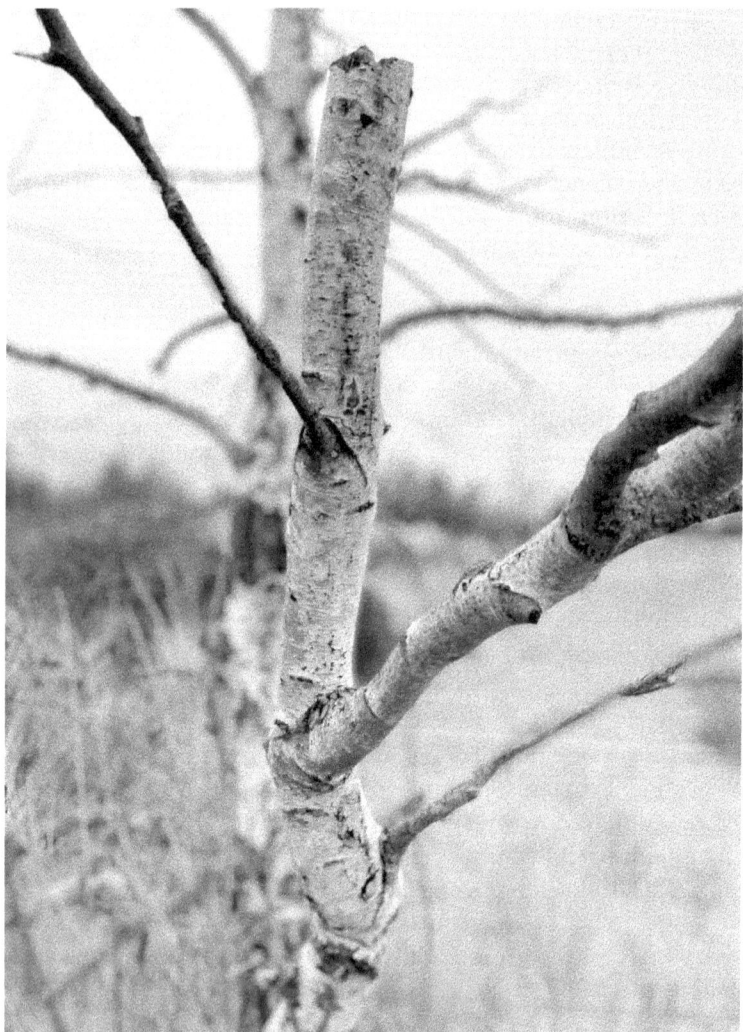

Section 3:
The General Welfare
18 Department of Labor & Related Agencies

- A Once Upon a Soon Time Tale

Attention, all, for the story you are about to hear is more comforting than you can imagine. "The General Welfare: Department of Labor and Related Agencies," under *The Pinkprint*, is reimagined as a champion for workers, prioritizing fair wages, safe workplaces, and the empowerment of unions. This vision rejects deregulation and market-driven policies that favor corporate interests, focusing instead on rebuilding the foundations of labor rights and ensuring every worker has the protections and opportunities they deserve. The reimagined DOL becomes a force for equity and economic security, putting the needs of workers above profit-driven agendas.

At the heart of *The Pinkprint's* vision for the Department of Labor (DOL) lies a bold commitment to workers, their rights, dignity, and futures. The reimagined DOL prioritizes strengthening labor protections and restoring the power of unions, recognizing them as essential advocates for fair wages, workplace safety, and equitable treatment. This vision acknowledges that workers are not just cogs in a machine but the backbone of the economy, deserving of respect and a seat at the table. By empowering unions, simplifying collective bargaining, and protecting workers from retaliation, *The Pinkprint* ensures that the Department of Labor becomes an unwavering ally to those it serves.

Unions take center stage in this transformation, with policies designed to revitalize their role in the workforce. The barriers that have long hindered unionization efforts, such as complex bureaucratic processes, employer intimidation, and lack of legal protections, are dismantled. *The Pinkprint* simplifies the unionization process, ensuring that workers can organize quickly and without fear. Collective bargaining rights are expanded, enabling unions to advocate for better wages, improved working conditions, and equitable benefits. These reforms create a level playing field where workers have the power to negotiate for their rights and employers are held accountable for treating their workforce fairly.

Equity is woven into every aspect of *The Pinkprint's* reimagined DOL. The vision prioritizes protecting the most vulnerable workers, those in low-wage jobs, gig economy roles, and industries historically plagued by exploitation. Policies address wage theft, misclassification of employees, and unsafe working conditions, ensuring that all workers are treated with dignity and respect. The DOL also focuses on closing pay gaps, particularly for women and workers of color, by enforcing equal pay laws and promoting transparency in compensation practices. This emphasis on equity ensures that labor laws uplift everyone, not just those at the top.

Workplace safety is a cornerstone of this vision. Under *The Pinkprint*, the DOL enforces stringent safety standards across all industries, from construction sites to corporate offices. Inspections are increased, penalties for violations are raised, and whistleblowers are protected from retaliation. Programs are launched to educate employers and workers on best practices for maintaining safe workplaces, fostering a culture of accountability and prevention. These measures go beyond compliance, they create environments where workers feel valued and protected, knowing their well-being is a priority.

The reimagined DOL also addresses the evolving nature of work in the 21st century. Policies are updated to reflect the realities of gig and contract work, ensuring that workers in these sectors receive the same protections as traditional employees. Benefits like health insurance, paid leave, and retirement plans are made portable, allowing workers to carry them across jobs and careers. This adaptability ensures that labor laws remain relevant in a rapidly changing economy, providing security and stability to workers regardless of how they earn their living.

Education and training programs play a vital role in *The Pinkprint's* vision for the DOL. Investments are directed toward workforce development initiatives that prepare workers for emerging industries, such as renewable energy and technology. Apprenticeships, vocational training, and upskilling programs are expanded, creating pathways for workers to transition into higher-paying, stable careers. Special attention is given to underserved communities, ensuring that opportunities are accessible to everyone, not just a privileged few. By investing in education and training, the DOL empowers workers to adapt and thrive in a dynamic economy.

Transparency and accountability are fundamental to this reimagined DOL. The Department operates with openness, regularly reporting on its enforcement actions, policy outcomes, and progress toward its goals. Employers who violate labor laws are held publicly accountable, sending a clear message that exploitation will not be tolerated. Workers are encouraged to report violations without fear of retaliation, knowing that their voices will be heard and their rights upheld. This commitment to transparency strengthens trust between the DOL and the public, reinforcing its role as a protector of workers.

Economic resilience is a natural outcome of these reforms. By improving wages, ensuring safe workplaces, and promoting equitable labor practices, the DOL helps create a stable and productive workforce. Workers with fair pay and secure benefits contribute more to their local economies, driving growth and reducing reliance on social safety nets. Employers, in turn, benefit from lower turnover rates, higher employee satisfaction, and increased productivity. This symbiotic relationship demonstrates that prioritizing workers is not just a moral imperative but also an economic one.

Ultimately, *The Pinkprint* transforms the Department of Labor into a champion of fairness, opportunity, and progress. It rejects the profit-driven, deregulated model of the past and builds a system where workers are empowered to shape their own futures. By prioritizing unions, equity, and innovation, the DOL ensures that labor laws reflect the values of a just and inclusive society. This vision moves beyond simply enforcing rules, it creates a labor landscape where workers are partners in building a better economy and a brighter future.

When labor was strong, the American middle class thrived, and the dignity of work was a cornerstone of the nation's progress. Union power didn't just protect workers, it uplifted entire communities, ensuring fair wages, workplace safety, and the promise of a better future for all.

Section 3:
The General Welfare
19 Department of Transportation
Yes, We can Have Nice Things- Like High Speed Rail

- A Once Upon a Soon Time Tale

Come closer, everyone, because what you are about to learn is titillating beyond belief. Under *The Pinkprint*, the Department of Transportation (DOT) is reimagined as a force for equitable, sustainable, and community-centered mobility. Rejecting deregulation and privatization, this vision prioritizes public safety, accessibility, and environmental stewardship, ensuring that transportation systems serve the needs of all Americans rather than corporate interests. The reimagined DOT focuses on connecting underserved communities, modernizing infrastructure, and creating a transportation network that is safe, reliable, and sustainable for generations to come.

At the core of *The Pinkprint's* transformation of the Department of Transportation (DOT) lies a commitment to universal access. This vision ensures that transportation is not a privilege for the affluent or urban dwellers but a public right that connects every person, regardless of geography or income, to the opportunities they need to thrive. *The Pinkprint* prioritizes investments in public transit systems that bridge gaps for rural and low-income communities, providing seamless access to education, healthcare, and jobs. Projects focus on expanding bus routes and rail lines, making fares affordable, and improving accessibility for people with disabilities. By addressing decades of neglect in underserved areas, the reimagined DOT becomes a driving force in creating a transportation system that truly serves all.

This vision draws inspiration from the bold ambition and ingenuity seen in other advanced nations, where transformative infrastructure projects have redefined mobility. *The Pinkprint* champions large-scale initiatives like high-speed rail networks, connecting cities and regions with unprecedented speed and efficiency. These projects not only reduce travel times and environmental impacts but also symbolize a commitment to progress and innovation. Investments in modernizing infrastructure extend beyond high-speed rail to include

99

repairing and upgrading bridges, highways, and transit hubs. Resilient, sustainable, and forward-thinking, these efforts set the stage for a transportation system that meets the demands of the 21st century.

Public transportation, under *The Pinkprint*, becomes the backbone of American mobility. Investments in state-of-the-art buses, light rail systems, and commuter trains make travel more reliable and efficient. Rural areas, which have long been cut off from robust transit options, are prioritized to ensure that no region is left behind. Expanded routes and schedules, coupled with affordable fares, make public transit a practical option for millions. Urban centers see an infusion of resources to address congestion and improve the quality of service. By focusing on the needs of everyday commuters, the DOT reimagines public transit as a cornerstone of community life, fostering connection and opportunity.

Safety remains paramount in this transformation. The reimagined DOT enforces strict safety standards across all modes of transportation, from buses to airplanes. Increased funding is allocated for inspections, maintenance, and modernization of critical infrastructure to prevent accidents and failures. Technology plays a crucial role, with the integration of advanced monitoring systems and smart infrastructure that enhance safety and efficiency. These innovations not only protect lives but also rebuild public confidence in the nation's transportation systems.

Environmental sustainability is a guiding principle in every project. *The Pinkprint* DOT prioritizes investments in clean energy technologies, such as electric buses, hydrogen-powered trains, and solar-integrated transit hubs. Programs to promote biking and walking, combined with urban planning that reduces reliance on cars, help cut emissions and improve air quality. High-speed rail and expanded public transit reduce the need for short-haul flights and single-occupancy vehicles, making significant strides toward climate goals. Every initiative is designed with the health of the planet and future generations in mind, proving that sustainability and progress go hand in hand.

Economic growth is an inevitable byproduct of this transformation. Large-scale infrastructure projects, like high-speed rail and bridge repair, create thousands of well-paying jobs, revitalizing local economies. Workforce development programs ensure that these opportunities are accessible to workers from diverse backgrounds, providing training in construction, engineering, and renewable energy. The ripple effects extend beyond job creation, improved transportation systems attract businesses, enhance tourism, and boost property values, demonstrating that investments in mobility benefit the entire nation.

Community involvement is integral to the success of *The Pinkprint's* DOT. Public forums, advisory committees, and local partnerships ensure that transportation projects reflect the needs and aspirations of the people they serve. Urban neighborhoods, rural communities, and Indigenous lands are all included in the planning process, fostering trust and collaboration. This inclusive approach ensures that transportation solutions are not imposed from above but co-created with the people who will use them every day.

The reimagined DOT also addresses the legacy of inequity that has shaped America's transportation policies. Highways that once divided communities are replaced with green spaces and walkable neighborhoods. Underserved areas receive priority in infrastructure investments, correcting the imbalance that has long left rural and low-income populations without access to reliable transit. Programs to subsidize fares for those in need ensure that cost is never a barrier to mobility. These efforts reflect a commitment to creating a transportation system that uplifts everyone, not just the privileged few.

Ultimately, *The Pinkprint* transforms the DOT into a model of what transportation can achieve when it prioritizes people over profits. It demonstrates that America can have the infrastructure it deserves, safe, reliable, and sustainable systems that connect us to each other and the world. By investing in bold, ambitious projects and centering the needs of communities, *The Pinkprint* DOT doesn't just move people; it moves the nation forward. This is not merely a vision for better transportation, it's a blueprint for a more connected, resilient, and just society.

Section 3:
The General Welfare
20 Department of Veterans Affairs
Compassionate Veteran Care

- A Once Upon a Soon Time Tale

Listen up, folks, because the events you are about to learn about are calming beyond belief. Under *The Pinkprint*, the Department of Veterans Affairs (VA) is transformed into a beacon of respect, care, and equity for those who have served. Rejecting privatization and market-driven solutions, this vision reimagines the VA as an institution that prioritizes comprehensive, accessible, and high-quality care for every veteran. By focusing on the unique needs of veterans and addressing the systemic gaps that have long plagued the department, *The Pinkprint* ensures that those who served their country are not forgotten but celebrated and supported with the dignity they deserve.

At the heart of *The Pinkprint* is a commitment to reimagining the Department of Veterans Affairs (VA) as a beacon of comprehensive, patient-centered care for those who have served. This transformation begins with significant investments in healthcare infrastructure, ensuring that VA hospitals and clinics are modernized and fully equipped to meet the diverse needs of veterans. State-of-the-art facilities are not just built or renovated, they are designed with veterans' specific experiences in mind, from physical disabilities to mental health challenges. The focus is not merely on treating ailments but on creating environments where veterans feel respected, supported, and understood. Every facility becomes a sanctuary, where the nation's gratitude is translated into tangible, accessible care.

A cornerstone of this reimagined VA is its robust approach to mental health services. The staggering rates of PTSD, depression, and suicide among veterans demand urgent and comprehensive action. Under *The Pinkprint*, the VA becomes a leader in mental health care, offering expanded access to therapy, peer support groups, and evidence-based treatments for trauma. Suicide prevention programs are integrated into every level of care, ensuring that no veteran slips through the cracks. Trauma-informed care becomes a central tenet of the VA's mission, with every provider trained to understand and address the unique psychological impacts of military service. These efforts extend to addressing substance abuse, with accessible recovery programs tailored to the needs of veterans. This holistic approach not only treats the symptoms but also addresses the root causes, empowering veterans to rebuild their lives with dignity and purpose.

Support for veterans' families is also prioritized, recognizing the critical role that loved ones play in the healing process. The reimagined VA offers programs for family counseling, caregiver support, and resources to help families navigate the challenges of reintegration. These initiatives acknowledge that veterans do not exist in isolation; their well-being is deeply connected to the health and stability of their families. By providing this network of care, the VA fosters resilience and strengthens the bonds that support veterans through their journeys.

Workforce reintegration is another pillar of *The Pinkprint's* vision for the VA. Employment programs are expanded to include tailored job training, apprenticeships, and career counseling, ensuring that veterans have access to meaningful, well-paying jobs. Partnerships with employers across industries create pipelines for veterans to transition into civilian careers that align with their skills and experiences. Special emphasis is placed on supporting disabled veterans, providing accommodations and opportunities that enable them to thrive in the workforce. These efforts are not just about finding jobs, they are about restoring purpose and dignity, recognizing the immense value veterans bring to society.

Equity underpins every aspect of the reimagined VA. Recognizing that veterans from historically marginalized communities often face additional barriers to care, *The Pinkprint* ensures that the VA's services are inclusive and accessible to all. Outreach programs target rural veterans, women veterans, and veterans of color, addressing the disparities that have long gone unaddressed. Language accessibility, culturally competent care, and specialized programs for underserved populations ensure that no veteran is left behind. By focusing on equity, the VA becomes a model of justice and fairness, embodying the nation's promise to honor the sacrifices of all who serve.

The VA under *The Pinkprint* also embraces innovation, leveraging technology to enhance care delivery and accessibility. Telehealth services are expanded, enabling veterans in remote or underserved areas to connect with healthcare providers without the need for travel. Digital platforms streamline appointment scheduling, medical records access, and communication between veterans and their care teams. These innovations reduce barriers to care, making it easier for veterans to receive the support they need. At the same time, the VA ensures that technological advancements are accompanied by robust privacy protections, fostering trust and confidence in its systems.

Accountability and transparency are integral to this transformation. The VA operates with openness, regularly reporting on its progress, outcomes, and challenges. Feedback from veterans and their families is actively solicited and incorporated into decision-making processes, ensuring that the department remains responsive to their needs. Independent oversight mechanisms are strengthened, holding the VA accountable for delivering the highest standards of care. This commitment to transparency builds trust and reinforces the VA's role as a steward of veterans' well-being.

Environmental sustainability is woven into the VA's infrastructure improvements, aligning its operations with broader climate goals. New facilities are designed with energy efficiency in mind, incorporating renewable energy sources and sustainable building materials. These efforts not only reduce the VA's environmental footprint but also create healthier spaces for veterans and staff.

Ultimately, *The Pinkprint* transforms the VA into a symbol of what a grateful nation can and should do for its veterans. It rejects the profit-driven, market-based approaches of the past in favor of community-focused care that prioritizes compassion, equity, and excellence. By addressing the physical, mental, and emotional needs of veterans while supporting their families and reintegration into civilian life, the reimagined VA ensures that every veteran feels valued and supported.

Section 4:
The Economy
21 Department of Commerce
Total Prosperity Framework

- A Once Upon a Soon Time Tale

Gather around, for the story you are about to hear is nothing short of a dream. Under *The Pinkprint,* the Department of Commerce is reimagined as a champion of fair, inclusive, and sustainable economic growth. Rejecting deregulation and privatization that prioritize corporate interests, this vision places the well-being of small businesses, workers, and vulnerable communities at the forefront of economic policy. The reimagined Department of Commerce focuses on fostering innovation, strengthening local economies, and ensuring that the benefits of growth are shared equitably across all sectors of society.

The Department of Commerce, under *The Pinkprint,* begins a bold transformation to ensure that economic opportunity reaches every corner of the nation, not just the boardrooms of the powerful. This vision centers on small businesses as engines of innovation, community resilience, and prosperity. By rejecting deregulation and privatization that prioritize corporate profits, *The Pinkprint* establishes a Department committed to fairness, sustainability, and the empowerment of everyday Americans. This reimagined Commerce Department invests deeply in programs that provide accessible funding, mentorship, and resources to entrepreneurs, particularly those from underserved and historically marginalized communities. It redefines the role of government in fostering an economy that reflects the collective potential of all its people.

Small business support under this vision is comprehensive and proactive. Beyond grants and loans, the Department tackles systemic barriers that have long excluded women, minorities, and rural entrepreneurs from full participation in the economy. Tailored programs in financial literacy, business planning, and regulatory navigation ensure that aspiring entrepreneurs have the tools they need to succeed. Partnerships with local organizations amplify these efforts, fostering vibrant ecosystems where small businesses thrive.

By valuing and investing in these foundational enterprises, *The Pinkprint* helps to rebuild the economic fabric of the nation, making it stronger and more inclusive than ever.

Innovation takes center stage, with the Department of Commerce spearheading investments in emerging industries that drive technological advancement and tackle pressing global challenges. From renewable energy to biotechnology, small businesses are at the forefront of these efforts, supported by grants, technical assistance, and access to cutting-edge research facilities. By ensuring that smaller enterprises have a role in shaping the future, *The Pinkprint* breaks the monopolistic grip of large corporations and spreads the benefits of progress across society. These efforts position the United States as a global leader in innovation while reinforcing the principle that economic growth should uplift everyone.

Local economies gain renewed focus in *The Pinkprint's* framework. Rural towns, urban neighborhoods, and Indigenous lands receive targeted support to revitalize their economic infrastructure. Public-private partnerships encourage the development of co-operative businesses, community land trusts, and renewable energy projects tailored to local needs. This commitment to place-based development ensures that economic growth is anchored in the unique strengths of each community, creating jobs and opportunities where they are needed most. By supporting these local initiatives, the Department builds a robust foundation for long-term economic resilience.

Fair trade becomes a priority, redefining how America engages with global commerce. Trade agreements are recalibrated to protect American workers, promote sustainable practices, and ensure ethical standards are upheld. Small businesses are given tools to access international markets, leveling the playing field in a globalized economy. These balanced trade policies foster domestic growth while ensuring that global commerce aligns with the values of fairness and sustainability. Under *The Pinkprint,* trade is not a race to the bottom but a collaborative effort to achieve shared prosperity.

Economic equity remains at the heart of this reimagined Department of Commerce. Programs focus on narrowing the wealth gap by reducing wage disparities, expanding access to affordable capital, and encouraging employee ownership models that distribute wealth more fairly. By addressing structural inequities head-on, the Department ensures that economic progress benefits all Americans, not just those at the top. Cooperative ownership models, profit-sharing plans, and employee stock options become standard practices, reinforcing the idea that shared success leads to a stronger economy.

Sustainability is integrated into every facet of the Department's mission. Incentives for green practices encourage businesses to adopt renewable energy, reduce waste, and build sustainable supply chains. Small businesses are supported in transitioning to eco-friendly practices through grants and tax breaks, ensuring that they can compete in a global market increasingly defined by environmental responsibility. These measures demonstrate that economic growth and environmental stewardship are not mutually exclusive but complementary goals.

Transparency and public accountability ensure that the Department remains aligned with its mission. Open decision-making processes, regular reporting, and community engagement keep the public informed and involved in shaping economic policy. The Department becomes a true partner to workers, entrepreneurs, and communities, rebuilding trust in government's role as a force for good. This collaborative approach ensures that every policy reflects the voices of those it is meant to serve.

By prioritizing small businesses, fostering innovation, and ensuring fair and sustainable practices, *The Pinkprint* transforms the Department of Commerce into a beacon of possibility. This vision does more than grow the economy, it redefines it, creating a system that values shared prosperity and collective progress. The economy becomes a tool for building a better future, where every person has the opportunity to thrive and contribute to the nation's success. Through this transformation, America moves closer to becoming a country where the economy truly serves its people, not the other way around.

Section 4:
The Economy
22 Department of the Treasury
Common Wealth

- A Once Upon a Soon Time Tale

Alright, everyone, get ready, because what you are about to learn
will surprise you for sure. "The Economy: Department of the
Treasury," under *The Pinkprint* reimagines the Department of the
Treasury as a driving force for fairness, accountability, and shared
prosperity in America's fiscal policies. Rejecting the outdated
playbook of deregulation and tax cuts that disproportionately benefit
the wealthy, this vision shifts the Treasury's focus to addressing
inequality, fostering economic stability, and ensuring fiscal policies
work for everyone, not just corporate interests. The reimagined
Treasury Department serves as a cornerstone of an economy
designed to uplift communities, promote shared prosperity, and
safeguard the public welfare.

Central to *The Pinkprint's* vision for the Department of the Treasury
is a commitment to transforming fiscal policy into a tool for equity,
accountability, and shared prosperity. Progressive taxation serves as
the backbone of this transformation, addressing the structural
imbalances that have allowed corporations and the wealthiest
individuals to amass vast fortunes while contributing
disproportionately little to the public good. Tax reforms are crafted
to ensure that the system is fair and transparent, closing loopholes
that have long enabled tax avoidance and eliminating offshore
havens that shield wealth from accountability. By demanding that
the wealthiest pay their fair share, *The Pinkprint* Treasury redirects
resources toward investments that benefit the entire nation, such as
universal healthcare, quality education, and robust infrastructure.

Fiscal accountability under *The Pinkprint* is rigorous and transparent.
The reimagined Treasury Department institutes mechanisms to
track the flow of public funds, ensuring that every dollar is spent
efficiently and ethically. Regular audits and public reporting foster
trust between the government and its citizens, demonstrating that
fiscal policies are implemented with integrity and purpose. Wasteful

spending is curbed, not by slashing essential services, but by eliminating inefficiencies and redirecting funds to where they are most needed. This commitment to accountability strengthens the bond between the government and its people, proving that fiscal policy can be both responsible and compassionate.

The reimagined Treasury also takes bold steps to address inequality through innovative economic initiatives. Programs to support small businesses and local entrepreneurs are expanded, offering grants, low-interest loans, and technical assistance to foster economic growth in underserved communities. These investments prioritize regions that have been left behind by decades of economic policy favoring large corporations and urban centers, ensuring that rural towns and economically distressed areas have the resources to rebuild and thrive. By focusing on localized development, *The Pinkprint* Treasury fosters economic resilience and empowers communities to shape their own futures.

A critical pillar of *The Pinkprint's* approach is the elimination of regressive tax policies that disproportionately burden middle- and low-income households. Payroll taxes, sales taxes, and other flat-rate systems are restructured to reduce the financial strain on those least able to afford it. Instead, the burden shifts toward wealthier individuals and corporations that have historically benefited from an inequitable system. This shift not only makes the tax system fairer but also provides relief to working families, giving them greater financial stability and more opportunities to invest in their futures. The result is a fiscal policy that prioritizes people over profits, ensuring that economic growth is felt by everyone, not just those at the top.

Sustainability is deeply embedded in *The Pinkprint's* fiscal strategy. The Treasury leads efforts to finance a green economy, allocating resources to renewable energy projects, climate adaptation initiatives, and sustainable infrastructure. Green bonds and other innovative financial tools are introduced to attract investment in environmentally friendly projects, demonstrating that fiscal policy can drive both economic growth and environmental stewardship. By aligning economic incentives with climate goals, *The Pinkprint* Treasury ensures that the nation's fiscal policies contribute to a healthier planet and a more resilient future.

In addition to promoting sustainability, *The Pinkprint* prioritizes global economic fairness. The Treasury works to reform international tax policies, collaborating with other nations to establish minimum corporate tax rates and combat tax havens that drain resources from public coffers. Trade policies are revised to ensure that they benefit workers and small businesses, both domestically and abroad. By promoting ethical trade practices and advocating for global tax reform, the reimagined Treasury positions the United States as a leader in building a fair and inclusive global economy.

Technology plays a transformative role in the Treasury's operations. Advanced analytics, artificial intelligence, and blockchain technologies are deployed to improve tax collection, reduce fraud, and enhance transparency. These tools ensure that the tax system is more efficient and that resources are allocated where they are needed most. Digital platforms make it easier for individuals and businesses to navigate the tax system, reducing administrative burdens and improving compliance. The integration of technology reflects *The Pinkprint's* commitment to modernizing fiscal policy to meet the demands of a rapidly changing world.

Public engagement is a cornerstone of *The Pinkprint's* fiscal strategy. The Treasury actively involves citizens in the policymaking process, hosting town halls, soliciting feedback, and creating advisory boards that include representatives from diverse communities. This inclusive approach ensures that fiscal policies reflect the needs and priorities of the people they serve. By fostering a culture of collaboration and accountability, the Treasury strengthens its role as a public institution that operates for the collective good.

Finally, *The Pinkprint* transforms the Department of the Treasury into a force for equity, sustainability, and shared prosperity. Its progressive taxation policies, commitment to accountability, and focus on inclusive economic growth redefine the role of fiscal policy in building a just society. This vision rejects the notion that economic success is measured solely by GDP or stock market performance. Instead, it emphasizes the well-being of communities, the fairness of systems, and the sustainability of growth.

Section 4:
The Economy
23 Export-Import Bank
The Export-Import Bank Should Be Abolished
Inclusive Trade

- A Once Upon a Soon Time Tale

Folks, brace yourselves, because the tale you are about to hear will leave you in giggles. "The Economy: Export-Import Bank: The Export- Import Bank Should be Abolished," in *The Pinkprint* reimagines the Export-Import Bank (Ex-Im Bank) as a cornerstone of equitable global trade and economic opportunity. Rather than dismantling this vital institution, *The Pinkprint* seeks to transform it into a transparent, efficient, and community-driven agency that supports small businesses, fosters innovation, and promotes sustainable economic growth. This vision prioritizes expanding access to global markets for entrepreneurs and underserved businesses, ensuring that the benefits of international trade are felt across all sectors of the economy, not just by large corporations.

The reimagined Export-Import Bank (Ex-Im Bank), as envisioned in *The Pinkprint,* becomes a powerful engine for inclusive and equitable economic growth, breaking free from its history of favoring large corporations to focus on empowering small and medium-sized enterprises (SMEs). These businesses, often overlooked by traditional financing mechanisms, are the lifeblood of local economies and the foundation of innovation and resilience. By providing accessible loans, credit guarantees, and export insurance, the reimagined Ex-Im Bank equips SMEs to compete confidently on the global stage, transforming challenges into opportunities for growth and collaboration. This new approach prioritizes diversity, inclusion, and sustainability, ensuring that the benefits of international trade extend to every corner of the economy.

At its core, *The Pinkprint* transforms the Ex-Im Bank into a champion for minority-owned and rural enterprises, recognizing the unique hurdles these businesses face. Targeted programs dismantle barriers that have historically excluded these groups from accessing the capital and resources needed to engage in global trade. Initiatives include workshops on navigating international markets, mentorship programs that connect small business owners with seasoned exporters, and streamlined application processes to ensure ease of access. By focusing on these underserved communities, the Ex-Im Bank levels the playing field, creating a trade ecosystem that values equity as much as efficiency.

Sustainability is a guiding principle for the reimagined Ex-Im Bank. Investments are directed toward green technologies and environmentally responsible industries, positioning American businesses as leaders in the global push for climate-conscious economic growth. Financing for renewable energy projects, sustainable manufacturing practices, and eco-friendly products becomes a priority, incentivizing businesses to adopt strategies that align with the needs of a rapidly changing planet. By integrating sustainability into its mission, the Ex-Im Bank ensures that its impact is not just economic but also environmental, fostering a trade system that supports the health of the planet and future generations.

The reimagined Ex-Im Bank also focuses on fostering collaboration across borders, building partnerships that emphasize mutual benefit rather than exploitation. Trade policies are redesigned to prioritize ethical practices, ensuring that American exports meet high labor, environmental, and human rights standards. This approach not only bolsters America's reputation as a fair and responsible trade partner but also creates opportunities for shared prosperity with nations around the world. The Ex-Im Bank's emphasis on collaboration and integrity strengthens global relationships, creating a network of trust and shared progress.

Transparency and accountability are woven into every aspect of *The Pinkprint's* vision for the Ex-Im Bank. Clear guidelines and open reporting mechanisms ensure that the bank operates with integrity, earning the trust of both businesses and the public. Regular evaluations of funded projects assess their economic, social, and environmental impact, holding recipients accountable for delivering on their commitments. This culture of transparency builds confidence in the institution and ensures that its resources are used to benefit the many, not the few.

Innovation thrives under the reimagined Ex-Im Bank, which actively supports businesses working in cutting-edge fields like biotechnology, renewable energy, and advanced manufacturing. By providing the capital and expertise needed to scale these ventures, the bank fosters a new wave of American ingenuity that drives growth at home and competitiveness abroad. These investments create a ripple effect, spurring job creation, technological advancement, and community development. The Ex-Im Bank becomes a catalyst for progress, demonstrating that economic leadership can be rooted in both innovation and inclusivity.

The bank also addresses the challenges posed by predatory international practices, ensuring that American businesses are not undercut by unfair competition. It provides financial tools and protections that allow SMEs to navigate the complexities of global trade without falling victim to exploitative practices or economic coercion. By advocating for fair trade agreements and enforcing ethical standards, the Ex-Im Bank safeguards the interests of American workers and businesses while contributing to a more just global economy.

The ripple effects of this transformation are profound. As small and medium-sized enterprises thrive, they generate jobs, stimulate local economies, and contribute to the overall economic health of the nation. Rural communities that have long been excluded from the benefits of global trade are revitalized, and minority-owned businesses gain the resources needed to grow and prosper. These outcomes are not merely economic, they represent a cultural shift toward a more inclusive and equitable vision of success, where opportunity is not confined to a privileged few but shared widely across society.

In the end, *The Pinkprint* transforms the Export-Import Bank into a force for good, redefining its role in America's economic landscape. It becomes an institution that reflects the nation's best values: fairness, innovation, and a commitment to shared prosperity. By aligning trade policies with the principles of equity and sustainability, the reimagined Ex-Im Bank demonstrates that America can lead the global economy with integrity and purpose.

Section 4:
The Economy
23 Export-Import Bank
The Case for the Export-Import Bank
Empowering Global Trade

- A Once Upon a Soon Time Tale

Pay close attention, everyone, because what is about to be disclosed is pleasant beyond belief. "The Economy: The Export-Import Bank: The Case for the Export-Import Bank," reimagined through *The Pinkprint*, becomes a transformative institution dedicated to fostering inclusivity, sustainability, and shared prosperity in global trade. By prioritizing small businesses, ethical trade practices, and environmental responsibility, the reimagined Ex-Im Bank shifts its focus from entrenched corporate interests to empowering diverse entrepreneurs and local communities. Transparent operations and community-driven initiatives ensure that the bank serves as a vital resource for businesses navigating international markets while upholding the principles of fairness and accountability. This vision redefines the Ex-Im Bank as a catalyst for economic opportunity and global cooperation, advancing trade policies that benefit everyone.

Under *The Pinkprint*, "The Case for the Export-Import Bank" rightly underscores the importance of the Ex-Im Bank as a resource for supporting American exporters, but it stops short of addressing the institution's deeper potential to lead in economic inclusivity, sustainability, and innovation. *The Pinkprint* expands on this foundation, transforming the Ex-Im Bank into an institution that not only supports businesses but also ensures that its benefits extend to communities and industries that have long been excluded from the rewards of global trade. This reimagined Ex-Im Bank is not just a lifeline for exporters but a driver of equity and shared prosperity in the global economy.

Central to *The Pinkprint's* vision is the empowerment of small and medium-sized enterprises (SMEs), which often lack the resources to compete with multinational corporations in international markets. These businesses, which form the backbone of local economies, gain access to funding, credit guarantees, and export insurance tailored to their needs. Programs are designed with simplicity and accessibility in mind, ensuring that SMEs from rural areas, minority-owned enterprises, and other historically marginalized groups can fully participate in global trade. Workshops, mentorship opportunities, and technical assistance further equip these businesses to navigate the complexities of international commerce. By prioritizing SMEs, the Ex-Im Bank ensures that trade becomes a tool for widespread opportunity rather than a privilege of the few.

Innovation is another cornerstone of the transformed Ex-Im Bank. Recognizing the rapid pace of technological change and the growing importance of sustainable industries, the bank invests heavily in businesses working in sectors such as renewable energy, clean technology, and advanced manufacturing. These investments create a dual benefit: strengthening America's position as a leader in cutting-edge industries while addressing urgent global challenges like climate change. The Ex-Im Bank not only provides funding but also facilitates partnerships between small innovators and larger enterprises, fostering collaboration that accelerates progress. By aligning its mission with the needs of a modern, sustainable economy, the bank becomes a catalyst for both economic growth and environmental stewardship.

Transparency and accountability are central to *The Pinkprint's* approach. The reimagined Ex-Im Bank operates with clear guidelines and public oversight, ensuring that its resources are allocated responsibly and effectively. Regular evaluations of funded projects assess their economic, social, and environmental impacts, holding recipients accountable for delivering on their commitments. Open reporting mechanisms foster trust between the bank, businesses, and the public, demonstrating that the institution serves the collective good rather than entrenched corporate interests. This transparency builds confidence in the bank's mission and ensures that its operations reflect the values of fairness and inclusion.

The Ex-Im Bank also takes on a leadership role in promoting ethical trade practices. Policies are enacted to ensure that American exports meet high standards for labor rights, environmental protections, and human rights. By requiring these standards, the bank positions American businesses as ethical leaders in the global market, differentiating them from competitors who cut corners. This commitment to ethical practices not only enhances America's reputation abroad but also creates a race to the top, encouraging other nations to adopt similar standards. Trade becomes a tool for promoting shared prosperity and justice, not a means of exploitation.

Equity underpins every initiative of the reimagined Ex-Im Bank. Recognizing the systemic barriers that have excluded certain communities from accessing trade opportunities, the bank prioritizes programs that uplift underserved regions and populations. Minority-owned businesses, rural enterprises, and women-led companies receive targeted support, leveling the playing field and fostering a diverse and inclusive trade ecosystem. These efforts extend beyond financing to include capacity-building programs that strengthen the long-term viability of these businesses. By embedding equity into its operations, the Ex-Im Bank becomes a force for reducing inequality and expanding opportunity.

Environmental responsibility is deeply integrated into the bank's mission. Funding is directed toward projects that promote renewable energy, sustainable agriculture, and eco-friendly manufacturing. By incentivizing businesses to adopt green practices, the Ex-Im Bank aligns trade with global climate goals, ensuring that economic growth does not come at the expense of the planet. Green bonds and other innovative financial tools are introduced to attract investment in environmentally sustainable projects, creating jobs and driving progress in the green economy. These initiatives demonstrate that trade can be a force for environmental good, setting a new standard for responsible economic development.

The ripple effects of this transformation are profound. As SMEs thrive and expand into international markets, they generate jobs, strengthen local economies, and foster innovation. Rural communities and underserved regions, often left behind by traditional economic policies, are revitalized, creating a more balanced and inclusive national economy. The Ex-Im Bank's focus on ethical practices and sustainability enhances America's standing in the global market, building trust and partnerships that benefit all stakeholders.

Section 4:
The Economy
24 Federal Reserve
Monetary Prosperity

- A Once Upon a Soon Time Tale

Come near, folks, for the story you are about to hear is happier than you can imagine. "The Economy: Federal Reserve," under *The Pinkprint* outlines a vision for fundamentally transforming the Federal Reserve's role in the American economy. The Federal Reserve, reimagined through *The Pinkprint,* becomes a champion of fairness, transparency, and shared prosperity. Its role extends beyond managing interest rates and inflation to fostering a monetary system that prioritizes stability, opportunity, and the well-being of all Americans. This vision ensures that economic policies serve the broader public, not just the interests of a select few, creating an economy rooted in equity and resilience.

In this reimagined role, the Federal Reserve evolves beyond its traditional functions of managing interest rates and inflation, becoming an active participant in the fight against economic inequality. No longer an opaque institution serving financial markets and corporate elites, the Fed under *The Pinkprint* prioritizes the needs of working families, small businesses, and marginalized communities. This transformation redefines the Federal Reserve as a stabilizing force for equity and opportunity, shifting its focus from short-term financial gains to building a resilient and inclusive economy that works for everyone. The emphasis moves from detached monetary policy to deeply engaged, purposeful action that addresses systemic disparities and fosters long-term prosperity.

Central to this transformation is a commitment to transparency and accountability. The Federal Reserve has historically been criticized for its perceived insulation from public scrutiny. Under *The Pinkprint,* this changes. Decision-making processes are opened to greater oversight, with public forums and advisory boards that include representatives from labor, small business, and historically marginalized groups. This participatory model ensures that monetary policy reflects the diverse needs of the nation rather than the narrow interests of Wall Street. Clear, accessible communication about the Fed's goals, strategies, and outcomes rebuilds trust and ensures that the institution is truly accountable to the people it serves.

Monetary policy under this vision takes a bold, proactive approach to addressing inequality. Instead of narrowly targeting inflation and employment metrics, the Fed incorporates measures of economic justice into its decision-making framework. Interest rate policies are designed to support wage growth and reduce unemployment in communities that have historically been excluded from economic gains. The Fed's dual mandate of maximizing employment and stabilizing prices is expanded to include reducing income inequality and fostering economic inclusion. This broader mandate reflects a recognition that true economic stability cannot exist without equity.

The reimagined Federal Reserve also leverages its tools to promote financial access and security for underserved communities. Programs are introduced to expand credit availability for small businesses and households that have been historically shut out of traditional banking systems. Community reinvestment initiatives focus on directing capital to areas that need it most, from rural communities to urban neighborhoods that have suffered from decades of disinvestment. By ensuring that credit flows where it is most needed, the Fed becomes a driver of grassroots economic growth and empowerment.

In addition to fostering financial inclusion, *The Pinkprint* Fed prioritizes the stability and sustainability of the broader economy. This involves rethinking the relationship between the Federal Reserve and the financial sector. Regulatory policies are strengthened to prevent the kind of speculative behavior that leads to financial crises. Banks and financial institutions are held to higher standards of accountability, ensuring that their operations contribute to the overall health of the economy rather than posing systemic risks. These reforms create a more stable financial system that supports long-term growth and resilience.

The Fed's role in combating climate change also takes center stage in this reimagined vision. Recognizing the economic risks posed by environmental degradation, the Federal Reserve integrates climate considerations into its monetary policy and regulatory oversight.

Policies incentivize investment in green industries and penalize unsustainable practices, aligning the financial sector with the nation's climate goals. Research and funding initiatives explore the economic implications of climate change, ensuring that the Fed is prepared to mitigate its impact on vulnerable communities. This approach reflects a commitment to sustainability that goes hand in hand with economic stability.

Education and outreach are vital components of this transformation. The Federal Reserve, often perceived as an inaccessible institution, takes on a more active role in demystifying monetary policy and financial systems. Public education campaigns and partnerships with schools and community organizations ensure that individuals have the knowledge and tools they need to navigate the economy effectively. This emphasis on financial literacy empowers people to make informed decisions, reducing economic vulnerability and fostering a sense of agency in their financial lives.

The ripple effects of this transformation are profound. Workers see real wage growth as monetary policies support robust job markets and equitable income distribution. Small businesses, empowered by greater access to credit and stable financial conditions, become engines of innovation and local prosperity. Communities that have long been left behind by traditional economic policies find themselves at the center of a revitalized economy, with targeted investments and inclusive growth strategies fostering resilience and opportunity.

Finally, *The Pinkprint* transforms the Federal Reserve into an institution that embodies the principles of fairness, accountability, and sustainability. It moves beyond serving as a gatekeeper for financial markets to become a champion for the broader public good. By redefining its priorities and expanding its mandate, the reimagined Federal Reserve ensures that monetary policy serves as a tool for justice, not just stability. This vision reflects a belief that the economy should work for everyone, building a foundation for shared prosperity and long-term resilience. Through this transformation, the Federal Reserve becomes a true steward of economic opportunity, committed to creating a future where no one is left behind.

Section 4:
The Economy
25 Small Business Administration
Grow the Independent Spirit

- A Once Upon a Soon Time Tale

Lean in, everyone, Because this story is sure to make your blood run warm. "The Economy: Small Business Administration," under *The Pinkprint* presents a vision that aims to support and uplift small businesses, and actively dismantles systemic barriers and builds a truly inclusive small business ecosystem. *The Pinkprint* reimagines the Small Business Administration (SBA) as a champion of equity and opportunity, prioritizing the needs of underserved entrepreneurs, fostering innovation, and ensuring that all small businesses, regardless of size or location, have the tools they need to thrive. This vision rejects a one-size-fits-all approach, instead embracing tailored solutions that reflect the unique challenges faced by diverse communities and industries.

The reimagined Small Business Administration (SBA) under *The Pinkprint* shifts from being a mere provider of loans and programs to becoming an essential pillar of economic equity and opportunity. It centers its mission on leveling the playing field for small businesses, particularly those historically excluded from traditional systems of support. By focusing on accessible funding, tailored mentorship, and resources that address systemic barriers, the SBA becomes an engine of shared prosperity. This transformation ensures that economic growth is not concentrated among the privileged few but instead benefits every corner of the nation, creating a vibrant, inclusive economy driven by innovation and opportunity.

Accessibility forms the foundation of this transformation. The SBA introduces streamlined processes to eliminate bureaucratic hurdles that have long made its programs daunting for small business owners, especially those from underserved communities. Small businesses in rural areas, minority-owned enterprises, and women-led startups gain priority in accessing resources. Funding mechanisms are redesigned to ensure inclusivity, with microloans, grants, and low-interest loans tailored to meet the diverse needs of these entrepreneurs. This comprehensive approach provides the financial support necessary for businesses to launch, sustain, and expand, giving equal footing to those who have traditionally been left behind.

Mentorship and education programs under *The Pinkprint* take a transformative turn. Recognizing that knowledge is as vital as capital, the SBA invests heavily in creating mentorship networks and educational resources that equip business owners with the skills needed to succeed in a rapidly evolving economy. Industry leaders, seasoned entrepreneurs, and local experts are enlisted to offer guidance, bridging the knowledge gap that often hinders small businesses from reaching their full potential. Training programs focus on areas such as digital transformation, sustainable practices, and global market entry, ensuring that businesses are not only competitive but also prepared to adapt to future challenges.

Innovation takes center stage in this vision. The SBA actively supports small businesses in emerging industries, providing the tools and resources needed to lead in sectors such as renewable energy, biotechnology, and advanced manufacturing. Grants and research funding encourage bold ideas and foster collaboration between small businesses and research institutions. By placing small businesses at the forefront of innovation, the SBA ensures that these enterprises are not merely participants in the economy but drivers of progress. This focus on innovation creates jobs, stimulates local economies, and cements America's leadership in the industries of the future.

Local economies are revitalized through the SBA's commitment to place-based development. Recognizing that each community has unique strengths and challenges, the SBA tailors its programs to meet local needs. Rural areas receive targeted investments in infrastructure and connectivity to support small businesses, while urban neighborhoods see initiatives to revitalize commercial corridors and support local entrepreneurs. Community-based lending programs and cooperative business models are promoted, empowering local leaders to shape the economic futures of their communities. By investing in local economies, the SBA creates a ripple effect of growth and opportunity, ensuring that economic success is shared broadly.

Sustainability is deeply embedded in *The Pinkprint's* reimagined SBA. Businesses are encouraged and incentivized to adopt sustainable practices, reducing their environmental footprint while improving their long-term viability. Programs provide funding for energy-efficient upgrades, green certifications, and renewable energy integration, aligning small businesses with broader climate goals. These initiatives demonstrate that economic growth and environmental responsibility can coexist, positioning small businesses as key players in the transition to a sustainable economy.

Equity drives every program under *The Pinkprint's* vision for the Small Business Administration (SBA). The agency actively works to close opportunity gaps by addressing systemic inequities that have marginalized certain groups. Outreach efforts target underrepresented entrepreneurs, ensuring fair access to resources and support. Culturally competent advisors, language accessibility, and partnerships with community organizations expand the SBA's reach, creating a small business ecosystem that reflects the diversity and resilience of the nation.

Transparency and accountability underpin the SBA's operations, ensuring fair allocation of resources and measurable outcomes. Public oversight and open reporting build trust, while businesses receiving SBA support are encouraged to reinvest in their communities through mentorship and local hiring. This virtuous cycle of growth fosters stronger connections between the SBA, entrepreneurs, and the public, amplifying the agency's role as a force for economic and social progress.

The impact of this transformation is far-reaching. Freed from systemic barriers, small businesses create jobs, spur innovation, and enrich communities. Rural towns gain new vitality, and underserved urban neighborhoods experience economic renewal, with small businesses providing goods, services, and a sense of pride. By prioritizing inclusivity, innovation, and sustainability, *The Pinkprint* redefines the SBA as a champion of fairness and opportunity, empowering entrepreneurs to shape a brighter, more equitable future for all.

Section 4:
The Economy
26 Trade: The Case for Fair Trade
Collaborative Trade Vision

- A Once Upon a Soon Time Tale

Listen carefully, folks, because what is about to be revealed is deeply supportive. "The Economy: Trade: The Case for Fair Trade," under *The Pinkprint* envisions a different approach, one that prioritizes ethical practices, collaboration, and mutual benefit over isolationism and conflict. This vision for trade policy recognizes the interconnected nature of the global economy and emphasizes partnerships that uplift workers, protect the environment, and create shared prosperity across borders. It replaces zero-sum strategies with cooperative frameworks, ensuring that trade becomes a tool for building equitable and sustainable economic relationships rather than fostering division and inequality.

Sustainability is a guiding principle in *The Pinkprint's* approach to trade. The reimagined strategy integrates environmental protections into every agreement, ensuring that trade policies support global efforts to combat climate change and preserve natural resources. Tariffs and incentives are introduced to favor sustainable goods and services, encouraging businesses to adopt greener practices. Investments in clean energy, regenerative agriculture, and eco-friendly technologies are prioritized, creating markets that reward innovation while reducing environmental harm. By embedding sustainability into trade, *The Pinkprint* ensures that economic growth does not come at the expense of the planet.

Transparency and accountability are central to *The Pinkprint's* trade policies. Agreements are negotiated openly, with input from stakeholders across industries, labor organizations, and environmental groups. This inclusivity ensures that trade deals reflect the interests of the broader public, not just the demands of powerful corporations. Comprehensive reporting and oversight mechanisms hold all parties accountable for upholding the commitments outlined in agreements. By prioritizing transparency,

The Pinkprint rebuilds trust in trade policy, demonstrating that it can be a force for good rather than a tool for exploitation.

Workers are at the forefront of this reimagined trade strategy. *The Pinkprint* recognizes that trade policies must protect and empower the workforce, ensuring that economic globalization does not undermine job security or wage growth. Programs are implemented to support workers displaced by shifts in global markets, providing job training, education, and transition assistance to help them thrive in new industries. Trade agreements include provisions that prevent outsourcing to countries with exploitative labor practices, creating a global standard that prioritizes fair treatment and economic dignity. This commitment to workers ensures that trade benefits the many, not just the privileged few.

Local economies also benefit from *The Pinkprint's* trade policies. Rather than focusing exclusively on national metrics like GDP, this vision emphasizes the impact of trade on communities. Investments are directed toward infrastructure projects that support local exporters, such as ports, rail systems, and digital connectivity, enabling small businesses to compete effectively in global markets. Programs that connect local producers with international buyers create new opportunities for economic growth and cultural exchange. These efforts ensure that trade uplifts entire communities, creating a ripple effect of prosperity that extends beyond individual businesses.

The Pinkprint redefines the role of the United States in global commerce, shifting from a position of dominance to one of leadership through collaboration. Trade policies become tools for advancing shared goals, such as reducing poverty, addressing inequality, and promoting peace. By partnering with other nations to establish ethical trade practices, the United States fosters a global economy rooted in fairness and mutual respect. This collaborative approach not only strengthens international relationships but also creates a more stable and interconnected world.

Addressing past failures is a critical component of this reimagined trade strategy. *The Pinkprint* acknowledges the harm caused by previous trade policies that prioritized corporate profits over community well-being. Reparative measures are introduced, such as funding for communities that were devastated by factory closures or exploitative trade agreements. These actions demonstrate a commitment to justice, ensuring that the mistakes of the past are not repeated. By confronting these issues head-on, the United States establishes itself as a nation willing to learn, adapt, and lead with integrity.

Technology plays a transformative role in *The Pinkprint's* vision for trade. Digital platforms are used to streamline the export process, making it easier for small businesses to navigate international markets. Blockchain technology ensures transparency and traceability in supply chains, reducing fraud and promoting ethical practices. Innovations in logistics and transportation make global trade more efficient and environmentally friendly, creating new opportunities for businesses of all sizes. By harnessing technology, *The Pinkprint* modernizes trade policy, ensuring it remains relevant and effective in an ever-changing world.

The ripple effects of these policies are profound. Workers experience greater job security and better wages, as trade agreements prioritize fair labor practices and prevent exploitative outsourcing. Small businesses gain access to new markets, driving innovation and growth in local economies. Communities benefit from investments in infrastructure and education, creating a foundation for long-term prosperity. On a global scale, trade becomes a tool for addressing shared challenges and fostering cooperation, building a more just and sustainable economy for all.

Ultimately, *The Pinkprint* transforms trade policy into a force for good, demonstrating that commerce can be ethical, inclusive, and sustainable. By prioritizing workers, communities, and the environment, this vision redefines what is possible in global trade. It rejects the isolationist and confrontational approaches of the past, replacing them with a strategy rooted in collaboration and shared progress. Through this transformation, the United States leads by example, proving that trade can be a driver of equity, innovation, and global solidarity. This is not just a vision for better trade policy, it is a blueprint for a fairer, more connected world.

Section 4:
The Economy
26 Trade: The Case for Free Trade
Responsible Commerce

- A Once Upon a Soon Time Tale

Gather 'round, all, for the events that are about to be recounted are truly positive. "The Economy: Trade: The Case for Free Trade," under *The Pinkprint* envisions a trade policy that prioritizes equity, sustainability, and collaboration, transforming trade into a powerful force for shared prosperity and global progress. This vision ensures that trade agreements protect workers' rights, safeguard the environment, and create opportunities for communities to thrive. By fostering partnerships grounded in mutual respect and fairness, trade becomes a tool for advancing innovation and uplifting people across all levels of society.

The Pinkprint replaces unrestrained free trade with a framework built on fairness, ethics, and shared responsibility. This reimagined approach to trade prioritizes the rights of workers, the health of the planet, and the economic well-being of all nations over the unchecked pursuit of profit. Robust labor protections are central to this vision. Trade agreements under *The Pinkprint* ensure that workers in all participating countries enjoy fair wages, safe working conditions, and the right to unionize. These protections create a global baseline for labor rights, preventing exploitative practices and ensuring that trade supports the dignity and well-being of the people who drive economic activity. This focus on labor rights transforms trade from a tool of exploitation into a vehicle for empowering workers worldwide.

Sustainability lies at the heart of *The Pinkprint's* trade strategy. Agreements prioritize environmental stewardship, mandating sustainable practices across industries and penalizing those that degrade ecosystems or accelerate climate change. Tariffs and incentives are aligned with global climate goals, rewarding businesses that adopt renewable energy, reduce waste, and invest in green technologies. The Pinkprint's approach to trade turns commerce into a force for environmental progress, setting a standard for how economic growth can coexist with the preservation of natural resources. By embedding sustainability into trade agreements, *The Pinkprint* not only addresses the immediate needs of the economy but also ensures a livable planet for future generations.

Transparency and accountability are cornerstones of *The Pinkprint's* vision. Trade agreements are negotiated openly, with input from labor groups, environmental organizations, and community leaders. These inclusive processes ensure that the voices of those most affected by trade policies are heard and respected. Mechanisms for monitoring and enforcing compliance with trade agreements are robust and transparent, fostering trust among all stakeholders. Regular public reporting ensures that governments and businesses are held accountable for their commitments, creating a culture of integrity that permeates every aspect of trade. This transparency strengthens trust between nations and between governments and their people, proving that trade can be both ethical and effective.

The reimagined trade framework also prioritizes inclusivity, ensuring that small and medium-sized enterprises (SMEs) can fully participate in global markets. These businesses often lack the resources and networks to compete internationally, but *The Pinkprint* addresses these challenges head-on. Comprehensive support programs provide SMEs with access to financing, export training, and market intelligence, leveling the playing field and ensuring that trade opportunities are accessible to all. Special emphasis is placed on minority-owned and women-led businesses, addressing systemic barriers and fostering a diverse and dynamic trade ecosystem. By empowering SMEs, *The Pinkprint* transforms trade into a tool for widespread economic opportunity rather than a privilege reserved for large corporations.

Ethical trade practices extend to the treatment of natural resources and supply chains. *The Pinkprint* establishes strict guidelines for resource extraction, ensuring that raw materials are sourced responsibly and with respect for the rights of Indigenous communities and local populations. Supply chains are monitored to prevent human rights abuses, child labor, and exploitative practices. Trade agreements require transparency and traceability, ensuring that consumers can trust the origin and impact of the products they buy. By aligning trade with ethical principles, *The Pinkprint* redefines commerce as a force for good, fostering trust and accountability at every stage of the trade process.

Collaboration replaces competition in *The Pinkprint's* vision for global trade. The United States engages with other nations not as a dominant force but as a partner committed to shared prosperity. Trade becomes a platform for addressing global challenges such as poverty, inequality, and climate change, fostering partnerships that prioritize collective progress. These collaborative agreements reflect the interconnected nature of the global economy, creating systems where mutual benefit replaces exploitation and where economic relationships are built on trust and shared values. This approach strengthens international alliances and promotes stability, making trade a cornerstone of global peace and prosperity.

Technology plays a transformative role in *The Pinkprint's* trade policies. Digital platforms streamline processes for businesses, particularly SMEs, making it easier to navigate international markets. Blockchain technology ensures the traceability and transparency of supply chains, reducing fraud and promoting ethical practices. Innovations in logistics and transportation reduce costs and environmental impact, creating a trade system that is efficient, sustainable, and accessible. By embracing technology, *The Pinkprint* modernizes trade while ensuring that advancements benefit people and communities rather than deepening inequalities.

The economic impact of this reimagined trade strategy is profound. Workers experience improved wages and working conditions as labor protections become a standard feature of trade agreements. Small businesses thrive in global markets, driving innovation and creating jobs at home. Communities benefit from targeted investments in infrastructure and education, building resilience and long-term prosperity. On a global scale, trade becomes a tool for addressing shared challenges, fostering cooperation, and creating a more just and sustainable economic system.

Section 5:
Independent Regulatory Agencies
27 Financial Regulatory Agencies:
Securities and Exchange Commission & Related Agencies
Fair Finance

- A Once Upon a Soon Time Tale

Friends, hold your breath, because what you are about to hear will leave you in pleasure. "Independent Regulatory Agencies: Financial Regulatory Agencies & Securities and Exchange Commission & Related Agencies," under *The Pinkprint* envisions financial regulation as a cornerstone of accountability, transparency, and equity within economic systems. It strengthens oversight mechanisms to ensure that regulatory agencies uphold the public good, safeguarding consumers and fostering trust in financial markets. This approach emphasizes the importance of rigorous enforcement, clear guidelines, and open communication, creating a financial system that protects individuals and promotes fair competition.

In this transformed vision, financial regulatory agencies become more than gatekeepers of economic efficiency, they evolve into steadfast guardians of stability, fairness, and equity in the financial system. *The Pinkprint* recognizes that a truly resilient economy requires robust oversight that prioritizes transparency, consumer protections, and accountability at every level. No longer operating as detached entities that serve corporate interests, these agencies are reimagined as champions of public trust, working to ensure that financial systems benefit all participants, not just the privileged few. This vision transforms regulation from a bureaucratic hurdle into a vital mechanism for safeguarding economic justice and fostering shared prosperity.

Transparency is a cornerstone of this reimagined approach. Under *The Pinkprint*, financial regulatory agencies implement open reporting practices that make their operations and decisions accessible to the public. Complex financial instruments, opaque market practices, and hidden risks are demystified, creating a system where consumers, small businesses, and policymakers can make informed decisions. Regulatory decisions are communicated clearly, accompanied by data and analysis that illustrate their impact on the economy and public welfare. This transparency not only strengthens trust in the financial system but also prevents the kind of speculative behavior that has led to past economic crises.

Accountability is equally critical. Financial institutions are held to rigorous standards that emphasize ethical practices and social responsibility. *The Pinkprint* introduces mechanisms to monitor compliance with these standards, including frequent audits and real-time oversight tools powered by advanced technology. Penalties for corporate malfeasance are significant and meaningful, ensuring that violations are met with consequences that deter future misconduct. By enforcing accountability, regulatory agencies under this vision create a financial ecosystem where stability and fairness are prioritized over unchecked profit-seeking.

Consumer protections take center stage in this reimagined framework. *The Pinkprint* ensures that regulatory agencies prioritize the rights and interests of individuals over the demands of powerful financial entities. Protections against predatory lending, exploitative fees, and deceptive practices are strengthened, with new safeguards introduced to address emerging threats in digital finance and online transactions. Accessible resources, such as financial literacy programs and advisory services, empower consumers to navigate the financial landscape confidently and securely. By focusing on the needs of everyday people, regulatory agencies become allies in fostering economic security and resilience.

Collaboration is a defining feature of *The Pinkprint's* approach to financial regulation. Regulatory agencies engage with stakeholders across the spectrum, consumers, businesses, policymakers, and community leaders, to create policies that reflect diverse perspectives and needs. This inclusive approach ensures that regulations are fair, effective, and responsive to the complexities of the modern financial system. Partnerships with international regulatory bodies enhance global cooperation, addressing cross-border challenges and creating a cohesive framework for ethical financial practices worldwide. This collaborative spirit transforms regulatory agencies into hubs of innovation and problem-solving, fostering a culture of shared responsibility and progress.

Sustainability and ethics are integrated into every aspect of financial regulation under *The Pinkprint*. Agencies prioritize investments that align with climate goals and social equity, encouraging financial institutions to support renewable energy projects, affordable housing initiatives, and community development programs. Green bonds, social impact funds, and other innovative financial instruments are promoted as tools for driving sustainable growth. Regulatory frameworks discourage short-term speculation and reward long-term, socially responsible investments, aligning the financial system with the broader goals of environmental preservation and societal well-being.

Technological advancements play a transformative role in *The Pinkprint's* vision for financial regulation. Agencies adopt cutting-edge tools like artificial intelligence, blockchain, and data analytics to enhance oversight and detect potential risks in real time. These technologies improve efficiency, reduce costs, and ensure that regulatory processes remain adaptive in an ever-changing financial landscape. Digital platforms are also used to streamline interactions between agencies and stakeholders, making regulatory compliance more transparent and accessible for businesses of all sizes. This integration of technology modernizes the regulatory framework, ensuring its relevance and effectiveness in a rapidly evolving world.

The ripple effects of this transformation are profound. Consumers gain confidence in a financial system that prioritizes their interests and protects their rights. Small businesses, freed from exploitative practices and empowered by fair access to credit, drive local economic growth and innovation. Financial institutions, held to higher ethical standards, contribute to a more stable and sustainable economy. On a larger scale, the reimagined regulatory framework fosters global economic cooperation, reducing volatility and building trust among nations. *The Pinkprint* transforms financial regulatory agencies into beacons of fairness, integrity, and resilience. These agencies no longer serve as passive monitors but as active participants in shaping an economy that works for everyone. Through this transformation, regulatory agencies become essential partners in building a more inclusive and prosperous future for all.

Section 5:
Independent Regulatory Agencies
27 Financial Regulatory Agencies:
Consumer Protection Bureau
Accountable Banking

- A Once Upon a Soon Time Tale

Alright, folks, gather close, because the story you are about to hear is nothing short of uplifting. "Independent Regulatory Agencies: Consumer Protection Agency," under *The Pinkprint* envisions a fortified and proactive Consumer Financial Protection Bureau (CFPB) as a bedrock of economic fairness and security. This empowered institution stands as a vigilant advocate for consumers, ensuring financial systems operate with transparency, ethics, and accountability. By prioritizing the protection of individuals from predatory practices and deceptive schemes, the CFPB fosters trust and stability in the economy, laying the foundation for resilience and shared prosperity.

By prioritizing the rights of everyday Americans, *The Pinkprint* transforms the Consumer Financial Protection Bureau (CFPB) into a cornerstone of economic justice and fairness. This vision restores the CFPB's mandate to protect individuals from the predatory practices that have plagued the financial system for decades. Exploitative lending schemes, hidden fees, and deceptive financial practices are dismantled under this framework, replaced with transparent policies and accessible tools that empower consumers to make informed decisions. The reimagined CFPB is not just a regulatory body, it becomes a trusted ally for consumers, ensuring their financial well-being is safeguarded against systemic abuses.

A major pillar of this transformation is the reinforcement of protections against predatory lending. Payday loans, high-interest credit traps, and exploitative mortgage practices have long targeted vulnerable populations, leaving countless Americans in cycles of debt. *The Pinkprint's* CFPB introduces stringent regulations to curb these practices, imposing caps on interest rates and fees while enforcing clear and fair lending terms. Community-based financial institutions are supported to provide alternatives, offering low-interest loans and financial education to break the grip of predatory lenders. This approach not only protects consumers but also strengthens local economies by fostering trust and fairness in financial transactions.

Transparency and accessibility lie at the heart of this reimagined CFPB. Financial products and services often come with complex terms that confuse even the most diligent consumers. *The Pinkprint* ensures that all financial offerings are accompanied by plain-language disclosures that clearly outline costs, risks, and benefits. Digital platforms are developed to provide real-time comparisons of financial products, helping individuals make informed choices tailored to their needs. This transparency builds confidence in the financial system, fostering a culture of accountability among institutions that were once opaque and unregulated.

Financial literacy becomes a cornerstone of the CFPB's mission under *The Pinkprint*. Recognizing that informed consumers are empowered consumers, the bureau invests heavily in education programs designed to teach financial basics, from budgeting to understanding credit scores. Partnerships with schools, community organizations, and workplaces extend these efforts, ensuring that financial literacy is accessible to people of all ages and backgrounds. For underserved communities, where barriers to financial education are often highest, the CFPB works to bridge the gap through targeted initiatives that provide the tools and knowledge needed to build financial resilience.

Access to fair credit is another transformative focus of *The Pinkprint's* CFPB. Systemic inequalities in lending practices have historically excluded marginalized groups from accessing affordable credit. The reimagined bureau addresses this through policies that require lenders to assess creditworthiness using equitable criteria, moving beyond outdated and discriminatory systems. Programs are introduced to expand access to credit for minority-owned businesses, low-income families, and rural communities, leveling the playing field and fostering economic mobility. By ensuring that credit is a tool for opportunity rather than exploitation, the CFPB becomes a catalyst for long-term prosperity.

Enforcement is a critical aspect of this vision. Under *The Pinkprint,* the CFPB gains enhanced authority to investigate and penalize financial institutions that engage in abusive practices. Regular audits and real-time monitoring ensure that regulations are followed, while meaningful penalties deter misconduct. These enforcement mechanisms send a clear message: the financial system exists to serve the public, not exploit it. By holding corporations accountable, the CFPB restores integrity to an industry that has too often prioritized profits over people.

Innovation and adaptability are woven into every aspect of this reimagined bureau. The CFPB leverages technology to stay ahead of emerging threats in digital finance, from cryptocurrency scams to data breaches. Advanced analytics and artificial intelligence tools enable the bureau to identify trends and risks in real-time, allowing for swift responses that protect consumers. These innovations ensure that the CFPB remains effective in a rapidly evolving financial landscape, demonstrating that regulation can be both proactive and forward-thinking.

The ripple effects of this transformation are profound. Consumers regain confidence in a system that prioritizes their needs and rights, enabling them to participate fully in the economy without fear of exploitation. Small businesses benefit from fair access to credit, driving local growth and innovation. Communities that have been systematically excluded from financial opportunities experience revitalization, as fair lending practices and education programs empower individuals to build secure futures. These outcomes extend beyond individual households, creating a ripple effect of stability and prosperity across the nation.

Finally, *The Pinkprint* redefines the Consumer Financial Protection Bureau as a champion of fairness, accountability, and economic justice. It moves beyond the limited scope of traditional regulation to become a dynamic force for progress, ensuring that the financial system works for everyone, not just the privileged few. By prioritizing transparency, enforcing accountability, and fostering inclusivity, this vision transforms the CFPB into a model of how public institutions can drive meaningful change.

Section 5:
Independent Regulatory Agencies
28 Federal Communications Commission
Open Communication Networks

- A Once Upon a Soon Time Tale

Come closer, everyone, for the tale you are about to hear will fill your heart with happiness. "Independent Regulatory Agencies: Federal Communications Commission," under *The Pinkprint* envisions the Federal Communications Commission as a vital institution that safeguards democratic values while fostering innovation and inclusivity in the communications landscape. This reimagined FCC prioritizes equitable access to reliable and affordable communication services, ensuring no community is left behind. It champions free expression, media diversity, and technological progress that serve the public good. Transparency and accountability lie at the heart of this vision, positioning the FCC as a protector of consumer rights and a builder of a communications infrastructure that reflects the diversity and needs of society.

Rather than weakening oversight, *The Pinkprint* strengthens the FCC's role as a champion of fairness, accessibility, and innovation in the communications landscape. It reimagines the agency as a bulwark against corporate overreach, ensuring that consumers, not profits, are at the heart of telecommunications policy. By safeguarding net neutrality, fostering competition, and expanding universal access to affordable and reliable services, the FCC becomes a driving force for equity and opportunity in an increasingly digital world. This vision restores the FCC's purpose: to serve the public interest by building a connected, informed, and diverse society.

Central to this transformation is a renewed commitment to net neutrality, ensuring that the internet remains an open and equal platform for all users. *The Pinkprint* enforces strict rules prohibiting internet service providers (ISPs) from throttling, blocking, or prioritizing content based on payment or favoritism. This guarantees that small businesses, independent creators, and everyday users have the same access to digital platforms as multinational corporations. By preserving the internet as a level playing field, the reimagined FCC fosters innovation and creativity while protecting free expression and democracy.

Expanding access to telecommunications services is a cornerstone of *The Pinkprint's* FCC. Millions of Americans, particularly in rural and underserved communities, still lack reliable internet and mobile connectivity. This digital divide exacerbates economic and educational inequalities, leaving entire populations behind. The reimagined FCC addresses this disparity with targeted investments in broadband infrastructure, ensuring high-speed internet reaches even the most remote areas. Subsidies and affordability programs make these services accessible to low-income households, while public-private partnerships accelerate deployment and enhance reliability. This universal access policy underscores the idea that connectivity is not a luxury but a fundamental right in the modern world.

Media diversity is another critical focus of *The Pinkprint's* FCC. The consolidation of media ownership has led to a homogenous and often biased media landscape that fails to reflect the diversity of voices in society. *The Pinkprint* implements policies to promote independent and local media outlets, ensuring that marginalized communities have platforms to share their stories and perspectives. Grants and funding programs support journalism in underserved areas, revitalizing local newsrooms and strengthening community engagement. By encouraging a multiplicity of voices, the reimagined FCC ensures that public discourse remains vibrant, inclusive, and representative of the nation's diversity.

Consumer protections are at the forefront of this vision. The FCC becomes a watchdog against exploitative practices by telecom giants, enforcing transparency in billing, pricing, and service quality. Regulations require ISPs and mobile carriers to clearly disclose fees and terms, eliminating hidden charges and misleading contracts. The agency also cracks down on spam calls, data breaches, and privacy violations, ensuring that consumers feel secure and empowered in their use of telecommunications services. These protections reinforce the FCC's role as a defender of the public against corporate abuses, restoring trust in an industry that has often prioritized profits over people.

Innovation and competition thrive under The Pinkprint. The FCC promotes policies lowering barriers for small and emerging telecommunications companies, fostering a dynamic, competitive market. Spectrum allocation policies prioritize equitable access, preventing monopolies and encouraging innovative technologies. Startups and community-based ISPs receive support to provide alternatives to corporations, ensuring consumers have real choices. This competitive environment drives down prices, improves service quality, and accelerates advancements in technology, benefiting everyone from users to the broader economy.

The FCC also embraces sustainability, recognizing the environmental impact of the telecommunications industry. Policies encourage the development and adoption of energy-efficient technologies and infrastructure, reducing the carbon footprint of data centers, networks, and devices. Incentives for green practices and innovations align the FCC's goals with global efforts to combat climate change. By integrating environmental responsibility into its mission, the reimagined FCC ensures that progress in connectivity does not come at the expense of the planet.

Transparency and accountability guide every decision made by *The Pinkprint's* FCC. Public forums and advisory panels ensure that the voices of consumers, small businesses, and community leaders are heard in policymaking. Regular reporting and independent audits ensure that the agency operates with integrity and remains responsive to the needs of the public. This open and inclusive approach fosters trust and ensures that the FCC remains a vital and effective institution for years to come.

In the end, *The Pinkprint* transforms the Federal Communications Commission into a champion of connectivity, equity, and innovation. It creates a telecommunications landscape where everyone, regardless of income, location, or background, has access to reliable, affordable services. By prioritizing competition, transparency, and consumer protections, the FCC becomes a force for progress, ensuring that the benefits of technology and communication are shared broadly and fairly.

Section 5:
Independent Regulatory Agencies
29 Federal Election Commission
Legitimate Election Integrity

- A Once Upon a Soon Time Tale

Folks, get ready, because you are about to hear a story more
enjoyable than you could ever imagine. "Independent Regulatory
Agencies: Federal Election Commission," under *The Pinkprint*
envisions a clear path, reimagining the FEC as a vital institution that
safeguards electoral integrity, ensures transparency in campaign
financing, and strengthens public trust in democracy. This approach
prioritizes rigorous enforcement of campaign finance laws, equitable
access to the political process, and the protection of elections from
undue influence by wealthy interests or foreign entities. The
reimagined FEC defends the democratic process, ensuring that
every vote carries equal weight and every voice is heard.

The Pinkprint enhances the FEC's capacity to hold candidates,
campaigns, and political organizations accountable, transforming it
into a cornerstone of democratic trust. Under this vision, the FEC
gains the tools and authority needed to enforce campaign finance
laws with rigor and transparency, ensuring that the democratic
process is shielded from corruption and undue influence. These
reforms prioritize fairness and equity, creating a system where
elections reflect the will of the people rather than the interests of the
wealthy few or powerful organizations. This reimagined FEC serves
as a guardian of democracy, safeguarding the integrity of elections
and restoring faith in the electoral process.

Central to this transformation is a renewed focus on transparency.
Voters deserve to know who is funding political campaigns, and *The
Pinkprint* ensures that information is readily available, accurate, and
accessible. Enhanced reporting requirements mandate that every
campaign and political action committee disclose the sources of their
contributions in real-time. This level of transparency exposes dark
money and curbs the influence of anonymous donors who have long
been able to shape elections from the shadows. Digital platforms
make this data publicly available and easy to understand,

empowering voters to make informed decisions based on clear, unbiased information. This commitment to openness shines a light on the financial workings of campaigns, ensuring that electoral outcomes are shaped by the people, not hidden agendas.

The reimagined FEC strengthens its enforcement mechanisms, addressing the pervasive issue of campaign finance violations that have often gone unchecked. *The Pinkprint* grants the agency power to investigate allegations swiftly and impartially, supported by advanced technology and enhanced staffing. Violators face meaningful penalties, including fines and disqualifications, ensuring the rules of the democratic process are respected and upheld. These enforcement actions send a clear message: no candidate or organization is above the law, and the integrity of elections will not be compromised. By holding those in power accountable, the FEC restores public confidence in a system many view as rigged or ineffective.

Equity in political participation is another cornerstone of *The Pinkprint's* FEC. The agency works to level the playing field, ensuring all candidates, regardless of financial backing, have a fair chance to compete. Public funding initiatives provide resources to grassroots campaigns and independent candidates, reducing reliance on wealthy donors and corporate interests. Limits on campaign contributions and expenditures are reintroduced and rigorously enforced, preventing a small elite from dominating the political discourse. By prioritizing equity, the FEC ensures elections reflect a diversity of voices and ideas, enriching the democratic process and fostering genuine competition.

Safeguarding elections from foreign interference and undue influence is also a priority. *The Pinkprint* equips the FEC with the resources and partnerships needed to address modern threats to electoral integrity, from cyberattacks to misinformation campaigns. Collaborative efforts with intelligence agencies and technology companies ensure that elections are protected from external manipulation, while stricter regulations on foreign donations close loopholes that have been exploited in the past. These measures not only protect the sanctity of the ballot box but also reaffirm the independence and sovereignty of American democracy.

Technology plays a transformative role in *The Pinkprint's* vision for the FEC. Digital tools streamline the reporting and monitoring processes, reducing bureaucratic inefficiencies and enabling real-time oversight. Advanced analytics identify patterns of misconduct, allowing the agency to address violations before they undermine electoral outcomes. Online platforms enhance voter engagement by providing clear, accessible information about candidates, campaign finances, and policy positions. This integration of technology modernizes the FEC, ensuring it remains effective and responsive in an era of rapid change.

Education and outreach are critical components of *The Pinkprint's* FEC. The agency works to demystify campaign finance laws and the electoral process, empowering voters to engage fully and confidently. Public campaigns emphasize the importance of transparency, accountability, and participation, fostering a culture of civic responsibility. In schools, civic education programs teach students about the role of the FEC and the importance of fair elections, preparing the next generation to uphold democratic values. This emphasis on education ensures the public remains informed and engaged, creating a resilient democracy built on active participation.

The ripple effects of these reforms are profound. Voters regain trust in a system that prioritizes fairness and transparency, participating in elections with renewed confidence. Candidates and campaigns operate within a framework valuing integrity and accountability, elevating the quality of political discourse. Communities historically marginalized in the political process find their voices amplified through fair policies and public funding initiatives. These changes strengthen the democratic fabric of the nation, ensuring elections reflect the collective will.

Ultimately, *The Pinkprint* transforms the Federal Election Commission into a pillar of trust, fairness, and accountability. By prioritizing transparency, enforcing accountability, and fostering fairness, this vision redefines the FEC as a guardian of democracy. It ensures elections remain free, fair, and inclusive, protecting the voice and will of every voter. Through these reforms, the FEC becomes more than a regulatory agency, it becomes a symbol of the nation's commitment to a democracy that works for all.

Section 5:
Independent Regulatory Agencies
30 Federal Trade Commission
Trustworthy Market Systems

- A Once Upon a Soon Time Tale

Gather 'round, friends, the account that is about to be revealed will send butterflies up your spine. "Independent Regulatory Agencies: Federal Trade Commission," under *The Pinkprint* reimagines the FTC as a powerful defender of consumer rights and market fairness. This vision enhances the agency's regulatory authority and enforcement capabilities, ensuring that corporations are held accountable, competition remains robust, and consumers are protected from exploitation. The reimagined FTC becomes a cornerstone of economic integrity, promoting transparency, innovation, and equitable opportunities in the marketplace.

Rather than weakening oversight, *The Pinkprint* empowers the Federal Trade Commission to take a proactive, assertive role in safeguarding consumers and ensuring fair competition in the marketplace. The reimagined FTC is equipped with enhanced authority and resources, enabling it to address anti-competitive practices, deceptive advertising, and exploitative behaviors with the rigor and efficiency demanded by the modern economy. Under this vision, the FTC no longer merely reacts to market abuses; it anticipates and prevents them, fostering an economic landscape that prioritizes fairness, accountability, and opportunity for all.

At the heart of this transformation is a commitment to rooting out anti-competitive practices that stifle innovation and harm consumers. The FTC under *The Pinkprint* takes a zero-tolerance approach to monopolistic behaviors and market consolidation that erode competition. Mergers and acquisitions are scrutinized with precision, ensuring that corporate growth does not come at the expense of smaller businesses or market diversity. When companies engage in price fixing, collusion, or other anti-competitive actions, the FTC imposes swift and meaningful penalties, sending a clear message that the market must remain a space of fair opportunity. By leveling the playing field, the FTC fosters an environment where innovation flourishes and consumers benefit from diverse choices and competitive pricing.

Deceptive advertising, long a bane of consumer trust, is another critical focus. *The Pinkprint's* FTC introduces stringent regulations to ensure that advertisements and marketing campaigns are truthful and transparent. Claims about products and services must be backed by verifiable evidence, and failure to comply results in significant fines and public accountability. The agency also prioritizes consumer education, launching campaigns to help individuals identify and avoid scams and misleading promotions. This dual approach of enforcement and education builds a marketplace where trust is restored, empowering consumers to make informed decisions without fear of manipulation.

Exploitative practices, particularly those targeting vulnerable populations, are aggressively tackled by the reimagined FTC. Predatory lending schemes, hidden fees, and exploitative subscription models are met with strict regulation and oversight. The agency establishes a dedicated task force to investigate industries that have historically preyed on low-income individuals, seniors, and marginalized communities, ensuring that protections extend to those most in need. These efforts reflect *The Pinkprint's* broader commitment to economic justice, making clear that exploitation has no place in a fair and equitable market.

Transparency is a cornerstone of *The Pinkprint's* approach to the FTC. The agency's processes and decisions are made accessible to the public, fostering accountability and trust. Businesses are required to disclose terms and conditions in clear, understandable language, eliminating the fine print that has long obscured critical information. Consumers are provided with digital tools to compare services, evaluate company practices, and file complaints with ease. These measures ensure that the marketplace operates openly, allowing consumers to engage confidently and without hesitation.

Technology plays a pivotal role in modernizing the FTC under *The Pinkprint.* Advanced analytics and artificial intelligence are employed to detect patterns of abuse and identify emerging threats in real time. Digital platforms streamline reporting and enforcement, enabling the agency to respond swiftly to violations. The FTC also collaborates with tech companies and international organizations to address cross-border challenges, such as data breaches and online scams, creating a global framework for consumer protection. By embracing technology, the reimagined FTC ensures it remains effective and adaptable in an increasingly complex and interconnected economy.

The economic impact of these reforms is profound. Small businesses thrive in a competitive environment free from monopolistic dominance, driving innovation and local economic growth. Consumers regain trust in a system that prioritizes their rights and protects them from harm. Communities benefit from equitable access to fair products and services, fostering financial stability and opportunity. These ripple effects create a stronger, more inclusive economy, proving that robust regulation and consumer advocacy are not barriers to growth but catalysts for progress.

Ultimately, *The Pinkprint* transforms the FTC into a guardian of trust, accountability, and equity in the economy. It redefines the agency's mission to ensure that markets serve the many, not the privileged few, and that every participant, businesses and consumers alike, operates on fair and ethical terms. By prioritizing transparency, enforcing accountability, and championing consumer rights, this vision proves that a thriving economy can also be a just one. Through these reforms, the FTC becomes not just a regulatory body but a symbol of economic integrity, ensuring that the marketplace remains a cornerstone of opportunity, fairness, and shared prosperity.

The TIDE it is a Turning!

Attention, everyone, last chance, the story does come to an end, for better and better. The TIDE is a Turning closes with a vision for America's future that is bold, transformative, and rooted in justice. It rejects the regressive strategies outlined in the Theocratic Heritage Foundation's Project 2025 version, which seek to reshape the nation through aggressive deregulation, diminished government oversight, and narrow conservative principles. Instead, The Pinkprint offers a pathway to genuine renewal, one that prioritizes social equity, environmental sustainability, and economic stability. Far from fraught with risks, this vision embraces the strength of collective action, innovation, and inclusivity to build a country where progress uplifts everyone, not just the privileged few. While the original Project 2025 rhetoric cloaks dangerous proposals in optimism, The Pinkprint is unapologetically transparent: America's renewal lies in advancing fairness, protecting the planet, and empowering its people.

Looking back on the vision laid out in *The Pinkprint,* we see the stark contrast between a government designed to uplift and empower its people and the regressive blueprint of Project 2025, which clings to systems of power that perpetuate inequality and oppression. The progressive transformation of each government department outlined here reflects a commitment to equity, sustainability, and innovation, a government truly of, by, and for the people. Yet, as we confront the challenges of our time, we must also recognize the truth: Congress, as it exists today, has become not only obsolete but actively harmful to the future we are building. The combination of modern technology and the repeated failures of Congress to act in the interest of the people make it clear that we can, and must, move beyond reliance on this antiquated institution.

Technology has transformed every aspect of our lives, from how we communicate to how we work, learn, and organize. It has made the world smaller, information more accessible, and collaboration more efficient. Yet our governance remains stuck in a bygone era, reliant on a system designed for horse-and-buggy times. Congress, with its gridlock, partisanship, and susceptibility to corporate influence, has failed to adapt. Instead of representing the people, it has become a tool for the powerful few, prioritizing the interests of donors and lobbyists over those of everyday Americans. This is not a government that serves the people; it is a government that hinders progress.

To build a modern future, we must acknowledge that Congress, as it currently functions, is not part of the solution but part of the problem. Its behavior has proven it untrustworthy, unable to act decisively on critical issues such as climate change, healthcare, and economic inequality. Time and again, Congress has shown itself incapable of rising above petty squabbles and vested interests to address the urgent needs of the people it purports to represent. It is not just ineffective, it is dangerous. The cost of inaction, of legislative paralysis, is borne by the most vulnerable among us. Every delay, every compromise, every deal struck in the shadow of corporate greed reinforces the reality that this system no longer works.

Modern technology offers us an alternative. Just as we no longer rely on the horse and buggy to navigate our cities, we no longer need a Congress that has proven itself incapable of navigating the complexities of a modern society. Decentralized governance powered by secure technology can allow for direct democracy, where citizens have a real and immediate say in the decisions that shape their lives. Blockchain technology, encrypted voting platforms, and participatory governance tools can replace outdated systems with ones that are transparent, inclusive, and accountable. Imagine a system where policy is shaped not by corporate-funded politicians but by informed citizens participating in open and equitable processes. This is not just a dream, it is a logical and achievable next step for a society that values progress over tradition.

Opposition to the status quo is not about dismantling governance but reimagining it. It is about creating a system that reflects the values of equity, sustainability, and collective empowerment. Congress, as it stands, does not represent the future we are building. It represents the entrenched interests of the past, clinging to power at the expense of progress. By defunding and decentralizing Congress, we free resources to invest in the tools and technologies that will allow for a truly democratic society. This is not about abandoning governance but elevating it, making it more responsive, more effective, and more reflective of the will of the people.

This shift will not come without challenges. Transitioning to a decentralized, technology-driven model of governance requires careful planning, robust security measures, and a commitment to inclusivity. But the rewards far outweigh the risks. A modern governance system can eliminate the bottlenecks and corruption that plague Congress, enabling faster, more efficient responses to the needs of the people. It can foster a sense of agency and engagement, empowering citizens to take an active role in shaping their communities and their futures.

The future we envision is one where governance is not a barrier to progress but a driver of it. It is a future where decisions are made transparently, resources are allocated equitably, and power is distributed widely rather than concentrated in the hands of a few. This is the promise of *The Pinkprint*, a modern, just, and sustainable society built not on the failures of the past but on the possibilities of the future. Together, we will leave behind the outdated systems that no longer serve us and create a governance model that reflects the best of who we are and what we can become. Congress has had its chance, and it has failed. Now, it's time to move forward without it.

The bottom line is that we can have nice things, if we choose to prioritize people over profit, collaboration over conflict, and sustainability over exploitation. A society that values equity, invests in its communities, and protects its planet is not a utopian dream; it's an achievable reality. The only thing standing in the way is the outdated systems and self-serving interests that cling to the status quo. When we dismantle those barriers and commit to building a future rooted in justice and compassion, we open the door to a world where everyone has access to the resources, opportunities, and dignity they deserve.

But here's the catch, you're going to have to get active and help us build this future. This isn't a spectator sport; it's a call to action. It's better to join us in shaping a world where we all thrive than to leave it to those who have proven time and again that they'll protect their power at our expense. Together, we can create the change we need.

Visionaries and Organizations

The Pinkprint draws strength from an enduring legacy of progressive visionaries and transformative schools of thought. Spanning centuries, these thinkers and movements champion equity, justice, and sustainability, providing the intellectual and moral backbone for our vision of a better society. Here are 25 key individuals and schools of thought whose ideas and activism shape and support *The Pinkprint*:

Folks to Reference

Harriet Tubman - Tubman's unwavering fight for liberation, opposition, and empowerment..

John Stuart Mill - Philosopher and economist, Mill's defense of liberty, social equality, and individual and collective freedoms.

Simone de Beauvoir - Author of *The Second Sex,* de Beauvoir's work on gender equality influences *The Pinkprint's* inclusivity.

James Baldwin - The writer and activist's incisive critique of race and class informs our fight on intersectionality and social justice.

Sojourner Truth - Truth's advocacy for women's rights and racial justice remains central to our vision for an equitable society.

Karl Marx - Marx's critique of capitalism and emphasis on collective ownership provides a foundation for our tomorrow.

Rachel Carson - Environmentalist and author of *Silent Spring,* Carson's work underscores our commitment to Mother Earth.

Emma Goldman - Anarchist and feminist, Goldman's belief in the power of direct action informs a future of collective action.

Thomas Paine - Author of *Common Sense,* Paine's advocacy for democratic principles and social equality.

Mary Wollstonecraft - A foundational feminist thinker, Wollstonecraft's demand for women's rights.

Ida B. Wells - Journalist and civil rights leader, Wells's fight against systemic racism.

Jean-Jacques Rousseau - Philosopher, advocate of the social contract, and proponent of equality and collective governance.

Chief Seattle - Indigenous leader, advocate for environmental preservation, and voice for land stewardship and cultural respect.

Albert Einstein - Beyond science, Einstein's advocacy for peace and social justice aligns with a holistic vision for humanity.

Victor Hugo - Author of *Les Misérables,* Hugo's compassion for the oppressed reinforces The Pinkprint's vision for a fairer future.

W.E.B. Du Bois - Sociologist and civil rights leader, Du Bois's work on racial and economic justice.

Gloria Anzaldúa - Feminist and writer, Anzaldúa's exploration of identity and cultural hybridity inspires The Pinkprint's inclusivity.

Leonardo da Vinci - Renaissance thinker and innovator, da Vinci's interdisciplinary approach mirrors The Pinkprint's vision.

Virginia Woolf - Her advocacy for women's autonomy and intellectual freedom reinforces The Pinkprint's feminist vision.

Sappho - Ancient poet whose celebration of love and individuality inspires The Pinkprint's embrace of diversity and self-expression.

Peter Kropotkin - The anarchist's theories of mutual aid and cooperation underpin The Pinkprint's community-driven governance model.

John Muir - Founder of the modern conservation movement, Muir's advocacy for nature preservation informs our vision.

In stark contrast to regressive entities promoting exclusion and inequality, The Pinkprint draws strength from progressive organizations and institutions committed to advancing equity, justice, and sustainability. These groups support economic fairness, environmental stewardship, and social inclusivity while fostering innovation and collaboration to address systemic challenges. Here are key organizations and movements actively working to shape a better, more equitable future:

Folks to Join and Support

ACLU (American Civil Liberties Union) - Defending civil liberties and fighting against systemic discrimination, the ACLU stands as a pillar for justice.

Planned Parenthood - Providing critical reproductive healthcare and advocating for women's rights and bodily autonomy.

Southern Poverty Law Center - Committed to fighting hate and seeking justice for vulnerable communities.

Earthjustice - A nonprofit environmental law organization that protects natural resources and advances climate justice.

National Education Association - Empowering educators and advocating for equitable public education for all children.

Greenpeace USA - Focusing on environmental preservation and renewable energy initiatives.

The Equal Justice Initiative (EJI) focuses on racial and criminal justice reform, and public education.

Amnesty International - Campaigning for human rights worldwide, this organization exemplifies global solidarity and action.

Union of Concerned Scientists - Merging science and activism to address climate change and public health.

Doctors Without Borders (Médecins Sans Frontières) - Providing medical care and advocating for global health equity.

Oxfam International - Fighting inequality and poverty, Oxfam's work is centered on economic and social justice goals.

Indigenous Environmental Network - Advocating for Indigenous sovereignty and climate justice.

Sunrise Movement - A youth-led movement to stop climate change and create millions of good jobs through a Green New Deal.

The Center for Reproductive Rights - Using the power of law to advance reproductive freedom worldwide.

Human Rights Campaign - Advocating for LGBTQ+ equality and inclusive policies that protect human dignity.

National Domestic Workers Alliance - Advancing rights and protections for domestic workers and caregivers.

NAACP (National Association for the Advancement of Colored People) - Fighting for racial justice and civil rights for over a century.

Fair Fight Action - Promoting voter protection and election integrity to ensure equal participation in democracy.

Food & Water Watch - Advocating for clean water, healthy food systems, and a sustainable environment.

Open Society Foundations - Supporting civil society groups worldwide that work on justice, governance, and freedom.

Common Cause - Advocating for transparent governance and accountability to restore trust in democratic systems.

Note on Kindness & Opposition

Kindness is often misunderstood. It is mistaken for fragility or seen as a concession in a world driven by power and competition. But in reality, kindness is among the most radical acts we can undertake. It is a deliberate rejection of the systems that thrive on cruelty and indifference. It stands in direct opposition to greed, fear, and division, reminding us that our humanity lies not in what we take but in what we give. Kindness, when woven into the fabric of a movement, transforms it.

True kindness is not passive, nor is it merely polite. It requires courage to engage deeply with others, to see their dignity even in moments of disagreement or opposition. It is the strength to listen, to connect, to understand the weight of another's struggle without judgment or dismissal. Kindness does not dilute the urgency of action, it amplifies it, ensuring that the fight for change is rooted in empathy rather than vengeance. It is not a retreat from conflict but a recalibration of how we approach it, a reminder that compassion is a force, not a weakness. In a fractured society, kindness serves as a counterweight, fostering solidarity and rebuilding trust in spaces where division has been weaponized.

However, kindness is not synonymous with acquiescence. It does not require tolerating injustice or excusing harm. In its truest form, kindness demands accountability. It calls out wrongdoing, not with malice but with a steadfast commitment to truth and fairness. It recognizes that transformation requires both grace and rigor, a balance between holding people responsible and creating the conditions for growth.

Within the framework of *The Pinkprint,* kindness is neither an afterthought nor an indulgence. It is a strategic and moral necessity, the foundation upon which we build a society that values equity and compassion. Kindness ensures that as we dismantle the old, we remain mindful of what we are creating in its place. It is not just an ethos, it is a guide, a commitment to building a world where humanity thrives not despite but because of our collective care for one another.

Kindness is not passivity, and our vision for a compassionate, equitable future does not mean we will stand idly by in the face of injustice. Opposition is the spine of progress, the unrelenting force that drives change against systems built to exploit, oppress, and degrade. To oppose is to refuse submission, to challenge power structures designed to hoard wealth and silence dissent. While others have hesitated, compromised, or been bought and sold by corporate greed and donor bribes, *The Pinkprint* commits to unyielding action. We will not be cowed. We will not be pushed aside. This movement will fight tooth and nail for the world we know is possible.

For decades, the political establishment has failed to demonstrate the courage and tenacity required to protect democracy and defend the rights of the many against the avarice of the few. Politicians, eager to preserve their power, often deliver rhetoric without substance, promises without action, and compromise without accountability. This is a failure we refuse to repeat. Opposition, as envisioned in *The Pinkprint*, is not empty defiance but strategic and deliberate. It is a commitment to confront those who seek to entrench inequality and injustice, using every available tool to dismantle their grip on power and replace it with systems that prioritize fairness, inclusion, and sustainability.

Make no mistake: opposition is not the antithesis of kindness, it is its most determined form. To oppose greed is to champion generosity. To challenge oppression is to uphold dignity. To fight against the destruction of our environment is to protect life itself. Our opposition is rooted in a fierce love for humanity and the planet, a love that compels us to act boldly and without hesitation. This is not a fight we take lightly. It is a fight we embrace with clarity and resolve, knowing that the stakes are nothing less than our collective future.

We will not be passive participants in our own destruction. We will meet the forces of greed and oppression head-on, with strategy and strength. Where others have faltered, we will press forward. Where others have compromised, we will stand firm. Our opposition will be the foundation upon which a just, sustainable, and inclusive future is built. This is not a moment to be meek; it is a moment to be unwavering. Together, we will rise, we will oppose, and we will prevail.

The Price of Principle

"You can't compromise with those who seek to silence you; freedom demands unwavering resolve."

In a small, divided town, a man named Simon owned a bookstore nestled between the church and the factory. His shop was a haven for diverse ideas, works of philosophy, literature, and dissent filled the shelves. But as whispers of the new fascist regime swept through the town, Simon began to see fewer visitors and more trouble.

The church leaders, emboldened by a rising tide of religious extremism, declared certain books dangerous. The factory, now run by a corporate giant with ties to the new fascist regime, started using its wealth to fund rallies calling for "traditional values" and "economic discipline." One by one, local businesses fell in line, their owners believing they could reason with the new powers, "work with both sides," and find common ground.

Simon, however, refused. "You can't reason with those who don't see you as equal," he told his neighbors, many of whom begged him to compromise. "They don't want dialogue, they want obedience."

One day, a representative from the factory visited Simon. He was young, clean-cut, and charismatic, offering Simon a deal. "Pull the banned books, add some inspiring titles from our list, and we'll sponsor your store. Everyone wins."

Simon stared at him, the weight of the offer clear. Accepting would mean survival, at least for now. But the cost was too great. "You're asking me to sell a future where no one has the right to read or think freely. You're not my ally, and I won't pretend you are."

Weeks later, Simon's store was vandalized, its windows shattered. His refusal had drawn a line in the sand. But the act sparked something in the town. Those who'd been silent finally spoke. They realized that siding with power meant losing everything.

There are no both sides when your freedom is on the line. Simon stood firm, proving that survival without principles is just another kind of defeat.

In Conclusion

The Pinkprint is a promise, not just of survival, but of something better, an end to fascism in America. It is a declaration that democracy is worth fighting for, that justice is worth the sweat of our brow and the courage in our hearts. This vision of America defies the grim narrative of those who seek to centralize power, strip freedoms, and return society to a time when oppression was law and progress was a distant dream. It offers a roadmap rooted in action, not platitudes, a path defined by the principles of TIDE: Target, Inspire, Disrupt, Empower. Each principle is a tool to dismantle the machinery of greed and inequality and to build a nation where fairness, not domination, reigns. Targeting the sources of oppression is the first step. This is not a vague ambition but a focused strike at the heart of injustice. Oppression doesn't thrive on its own; it requires funding, policy, and complicity. *The Pinkprint* takes aim at corporations that pollute the planet, underpay their workers, and funnel money into systems designed to disenfranchise the many for the benefit of the few. It demands transparency from industries profiting off suffering, from fossil fuel giants accelerating climate catastrophe to tech monopolies weaponizing surveillance.

But opposition to fascism requires more than outrage; it demands hope. To inspire is to breathe life into movements that can feel overwhelming, to remind people that progress is possible even when the odds seem insurmountable. Inspiration begins with stories, of communities coming together, of individuals rising to meet challenges, of triumphs large and small that show the way forward. It is found in art and music, in the collective joy of shared struggle, and in the humor that mocks those who wield power unjustly. Laughter is its own form of resistance, an antidote to fear and despair. *The Pinkprint* believes in amplifying voices from all walks of life, ensuring that inspiration is not the privilege of the elite but the shared spark of every worker, student, and citizen. This isn't about empty platitudes; it's about crafting a vision of a better world and inviting everyone to build it together.

Disruption is where movements find their muscle. Oppression thrives on order, on the steady rhythm of compliance, the quiet acceptance of unfair rules, the predictable cycles of unchecked power. Disrupting these rhythms is not chaos for its own sake; it is a calculated interruption that forces the system to reckon with its fragility. Strikes, boycotts, and coordinated walkouts remind corporations that their profits are not inevitable. Protests and sit-ins disrupt the comfort of those who legislate injustice from positions of privilege. Even small acts of defiance, a workplace slowdown, a consumer turning to ethical alternatives, a community staging a flash mob in front of a corporate headquarters, add to the cumulative force of change. Disruption is not a one-time event; it is a sustained pressure, applied strategically, that erodes the foundations of inequity and paves the way for something new.

And that something new is empowerment, the most essential and transformative principle of all. Empowerment is more than resistance; it is the act of building a just society to replace the one that failed us. It means returning power to communities through participatory governance, where neighbors make decisions about budgets, policies, and priorities. It means investing in mutual aid networks that bypass bureaucratic red tape to provide food, housing, and support directly to those who need it. It means creating public systems that are truly public, universal healthcare, accessible education, and wages that reflect the dignity of work. *The Pinkprint* also embraces technology not as a tool for surveillance but as an instrument for liberation. Secure apps enable grassroots organizing without fear of retaliation; decentralized platforms allow for direct democracy at scales once unimaginable. Empowerment is not an abstract ideal but a practical strategy for resilience, ensuring that the structures we build cannot be easily co-opted or destroyed.

The Pinkprint is not just a counterargument to regressive fascist policies; it is a vision for a nation transformed. It asks us to imagine an America where power flows from the people, not toward the powerful; where freedom is not conditional but universal, where progress is not a privilege but a right. It is a call to action rooted in the belief that change is not only necessary but inevitable when the tide turns. Together, we will rise, targeting injustice, inspiring hope, disrupting oppression, and empowering one another to create a future that honors the dignity of every person.

Stopping Project 2025, The Republicans, Christian fascism, and oligarchy in the United States requires an approach that addresses systemic corruption, promotes accountability, and strengthens democratic institutions. Here are some actionable strategies:

Campaign Finance Reform
End the domination of money in politics by overturning decisions like *Citizens United v. FEC* that enable unlimited political spending by corporations and the ultra-wealthy.

Support publicly funded elections to level the playing field for candidates not backed by wealthy donors.

Increase transparency in political donations to expose dark money influence.

Strengthen Antitrust Laws
Break up monopolies and limit corporate concentration in industries like technology, media, healthcare, and finance.

Enforce existing antitrust laws to foster competition and prevent corporations from wielding outsized political influence.

Tax the Wealthy Fairly
Close loopholes that allow billionaires to avoid taxes.

Introduce progressive tax reforms, such as a wealth tax, to redistribute resources and fund public goods.

Crack down on offshore tax havens and corporate tax avoidance schemes.

Empower Unions and Workers
Strengthen labor laws to protect union organizing and collective bargaining.

Raise the federal minimum wage to a living wage and ensure workplace protections.

Reduce the power of corporations to suppress workers' rights and benefits.

Rein in Corporate Lobbying
Restrict corporate lobbying efforts that prioritize profits over public welfare.

Mandate transparency and reporting for all lobbying activities.

Prohibit former government officials from working as lobbyists immediately after leaving office.

Support Grassroots Movements
Invest in local activism to build power from the ground up.

Support organizations fighting for voting rights, economic justice, environmental protections, and more.

Elevate voices from marginalized communities to challenge oligarchic systems.

Protect Voting Rights
Expand access to voting through measures like automatic voter registration, vote-by-mail, and extended early voting.

Combat voter suppression laws that disproportionately harm marginalized groups.

End gerrymandering and promote independent redistricting commissions.

Hold Leaders Accountable
Investigate and prosecute corruption at all levels of government.

Demand ethical standards for public officials and limit conflicts of interest.

Ensure independent oversight bodies are adequately funded and empowered.

Promote a Free and Independent Press
Support public media and nonprofit journalism that expose corruption and hold power to account.

Push back against media consolidation that limits diverse perspectives and independent reporting.

Educate the public on media literacy to counter propaganda and misinformation.

Civic Engagement and Education
Teach critical thinking and civic education in schools to empower future generations.

Encourage active participation in democracy through voting, activism, and community organizing.

Foster dialogue that unites Americans across political divides to focus on shared values.

Push for Systemic Change
Advocate for structural reforms, such as abolishing the Electoral College or expanding the Supreme Court, to make government more representative.

Strengthen laws preventing conflicts of interest between government and private enterprise.

Explore public ownership of essential services like healthcare, education, and utilities to reduce corporate profiteering.

Challenge the Narrative
Expose the myth of "trickle-down economics" and highlight how policies disproportionately favor the wealthy.

Frame economic inequality as a moral and societal failure that harms everyone.

Use cultural platforms to challenge the normalization of oligarchic power.

In closing, democracy is inherently messy and thrives on full participation to function effectively. To create the future we deserve, we must confront and remove the obstacles in our way: greedy, corrupt politicians, and laws and policies that favor the wealthy while harming everyone else. This requires collective effort and determination from all of us. Together, we can build a fairer, more just society that works for everyone. That's all, now let's get to work!

List of Prints

About the authors

The authors live removed.

Please feel free to burn part or all of this book, safely, as an effigy.